Britain's Railways
From the Air

Then & Now

Britain's Railways
From the Air

Then & Now

Aerofilms

IAN ALLAN
Publishing

DUNDEE

Then: August 1953
Now: 17 June 1998

Situated on the north bank of the River Tay estuary and nestling at the foot of a long extinct volcano, Dundee was and is an important industrial and maritime city. Famous for its three 'Js' — jam, jute and journalism — Dundee is, for railway enthusiasts, perhaps best known as being served by the Tay Bridge, the longest railway bridge in Britain and successor to the ill-fated structure that collapsed in 1879. The 'Then' photograph, taken looking eastwards, shows the railway provision dominating the foreshore on the west of the city with the docks beyond. At the centre of the photograph is the Caledonian Railway's Dundee West terminus station; alongside is the ex-CR goods shed whilst further south, and at a slightly lower level, is the ex-North British Tay Bridge station. The ex-NBR line can be seen curving away to the northeast and entering Dock Street Tunnel which passes under the harbour area to re-emerge at Camperdown Junction. In the distance can also be seen the terminus of the Dundee & Arbroath Joint Railway at Dundee East with the D&A Joint line stretching eastwards towards Broughty Ferry. Back in the foreground can be seen the ex-NBR goods yard. In the period before the Tay road bridge was constructed, there was a car ferry across the River Tay, evidence of which can be seen. Finally, the turntable and part of the shed of the ex-NBR Dundee Tay Bridge shed (62B) can be seen in the foreground; this shed lost its steam allocation in May 1967.

Dundee's first Railway was the Dundee & Newtyle, which opened to a terminus (long closed) at Ward Road, which was served by a tunnel under Dundee Law, and a link to the harbour. This line, originally constructed to the gauge of 4ft 6.5in, opened on 16 December 1831. The Dundee & Arbroath line opened on 6 October 1838. The Dundee & Perth line opened on 24 May 1847. The NBR arrived, courtesy of the first Tay Bridge, when the first train crossed the new bridge on 26 September 1877; the NBR's triumph was, however, to be shortlived, as part of the bridge collapsed on 28 December 1879. The new bridge opened on 11 July 1887. Following the arrival of the NBR, the D&A line became a joint NBR/CR line from 1 February 1880.

The scene at Dundee is dramatically different today, with the area now dominated by the approach roads to the Tay road bridge, which opened in the mid-1960s. Although the railway lines to Perth, Arbroath and across the Tay remain open, Dundee has been reduced to a single station. Dundee East closed on 5 January 1959 and Dundee West on 3 May 1965; in both cases the surviving services were transferred to Dundee Tay Bridge and the stations demolished quickly after closure (West in 1966). The ex-NBR Tay Bridge goods yard closed in the early 1960s, with traffic being transferred to the ex-CR Dundee West yard. Now known simply as 'Dundee', the station was considerably modernised in 1985 at which time the area was resignalled. Both the ex-NBR and ex-CR sheds are now closed; the latter surviving until the early 1980s. As can be seen, Dundee Tay Bridge station remains, although the approaches to it have been much rationalised. Of Dundee West there is now no trace and both goods sheds have also disappeared. Located in the harbour adjacent to Tay Bridge station is the preserved *Discovery*, which was used by Captain Scott for Antarctic exploration and which had originally been built at Dundee; the ship's preservation on the Tay has led to Dundee's modern slogan — 'City of Discovery'. **(A51263/675377)**

CONTENTS

First published 1998

ISBN 0 7110 2595 9

All rights reserved. No part of this book may be reproduced or transmitted in any form or by any means, electronic or mechanical, including photocopying, recording or by any information storage and retrieval system, without permission from the Publisher in writing.

© Aerofilms 1998 (photographs)
© Ian Allan Publishing Ltd 1998 (text)

Published by Ian Allan Publishing

an imprint of Ian Allan Publishing Ltd, Terminal House, Station Approach, Shepperton, Surrey TW17 8AS; and printed by Ian Allan Printing Ltd, Riverdene Business Park, Molesey Road, Hersham, Surrey KT12 4RG.

Code: 9808/

INTRODUCTION

Established in 1919, Aerofilms has been recording Britain's cities, towns, villages and landscape from the air for almost 80 years. In that time the company has amassed an enormous archive of more than a million images. Whilst the vast majority of these are of little interest to the railway enthusiast, there are many gems to be found that portray Britain's railways. This selection, drawn from the Aerofilms' archive, includes some 125 different locations from the length and breadth of the United Kingdom. Each of the 'Then' shots is an historic image — the earliest dating from the early 1920s the most recent from the early 1970s — that illustrate the railway infrastructure of the time. Each of these 'Then' photographs has been replicated, as far as is possible with the constraints of modern regulations and flightpaths, with a contemporary photograph taken specially for this publication.

In making the selection of 'Then' photographs, we have endeavoured to try and record most major cities, as far as is possible, and major railway centres. With a limited number of 'Then' shots permissible within the confines of the book, there may well be omissions; it may well be that no suitable 'Then' shots survive or that, by trying to achieve a reasonable geographical spread, we have had to make compromises. None the less, the illustrations that have been included do reflect the impact of the railways upon the British landscape over the past 170 years.

The Aerofilms company undertakes two distinct types of aerial photography. The first of these are 'oblique' shots, which portray the landscape from an angle. These photographs are idea for examining buildings and infrastructure and, for that reason, the vast majority of the photographs in this book are of this nature. In terms of the detail visible, a great deal will depend upon the actual height of the aircraft from the ground when the photograph was taken. In some, where the aircraft was closer to the ground, it is possible to identify precisely track layouts and even, on occasion, locomotive numbers. The more distant perspective, however, is ideal for permitting the relationship between various lines and stations to be appreciated better. The second style of photograph, the 'vertical', is used largely for the compilation of maps. We have only included a couple of vertical illustrations as, generally speaking, their usefulness to the enthusiast is perhaps not as great.

Examining these photographs one is struck by a number of conclusions. Firstly, how much land was occupied — even in the historic cities of, for example York and Chester — by the railways and by how much the railways have shrunk over the past 30 years. Secondly, and this is a comment of a more general nature, the considerable spread of urbanisation over the decades is all too evident in the 'Now' photographs; as this text is being completed the government has just announced that 'only' 40% of the estimated 5 million new households will be permitted on greenfield sites in the future. By my reckoning, that still means that the countryside — or more likely the threatened green belts around the major conurbations — will still have to accommodate some 2 million dwellings and so, if this book were to be undertaken again in a further 30 years, much of the greenery evident here will have disappeared.

We hope that you will find as much interest in these comparison photographs as we did in selecting them and compiling the captions.

Front cover: **Preston.**
Back cover: **Folkestone.**
Previous pages: **Liverpool.**

Acknowledgements

We would like to thank the staff at Aerofilms, without whose assistance this project would not have been possible. Copies of all Aerofilms photographs are available from the company, by quoting the reference number, at the company's offices: Gate Studios, Station Road, Borehamwood, Hertfordshire WD6 1EJ. Tel: 0181 207 0666

ALNWICK

Then: 5 October 1932
Now: 3 November 1997

With Alnwick Castle, one of the Duke of Northumberland's homes, dominating the skyline, the impressive scale of the station serving this Northumberland town is evident. Alnwick was effectively the terminus of two branches, both operated by the North Eastern Railway, that served Alnmouth (opened officially on 5 August 1850) and to Coldstream via Ilderton (which opened on 5 September 1887). The impressive station, designed by William Bell (who also designed the stations at Darlington and Hull Paragon), was opened in 1887 at the same time as the line to Coldstream. Whilst the station was grandiose, the time table was perhaps less generous with less than 20 return workings between Alnmouth and Alnwick over the three-mile branch in 1939. Already, by

the date of the 'Then' photograph, passenger services over the line to Coldstream had been withdrawn, these ceasing on 22 September 1930.

In late 1997, whilst the station has lost its platforms, it is still recognisable as the building that Bell designed more than 110 years ago. Passenger services on the line between Alnwick and Alnmouth were withdrawn on 29 January 1968. Freight over the section of line from Alnwick to Ilderton had already been withdrawn (on 2 March 1953). Alnwick was to lose its last rail connection on 7 October 1968 when freight was withdrawn from the branch to Alnmouth. As can be seen, much of the trackbed for the line towards Coldstream is extant and it is possible to see remains of the Alnmouth branch, although there are modern buildings at the actual junction. Thirty years on, there is now a group campaigning for the branch to Alnmouth to be reopened; who knows, in another decade a follow-up volume to this may be able to record rails once again serving this Northumberland town. **(40688/672611)**

ASHFORD

Then: 30 June 1969
Now: 8 May 1998

This view, looking north, shows the important junction at Ashford in Kent. In the foreground can be seen the four platforms of the station with the two through roads running between the two island platforms. From the station the line divides, with lines heading southwards to Hastings, southeastwards to Folkestone and eastwards towards Canterbury. North of the station, the line divides at Ashford B Junction, with the Maidstone line heading northwestwards and the Tonbridge line heading due west. Ashford West yard can be seen; this is accessed off the Maidstone line. Just west of the junction, the four tracks heading towards Tonbridge are reduced to two. Ashford

Works is not illustrated; it was slightly to the south of the area illustrated.

The first railway to serve Ashford was the South Eastern, which opened on 1 December 1842; the route was extended to Folkestone on 28 June 1843. The route to Maidstone opened on 1 July 1844; this was followed by that to Canterbury, which opened on 6 February 1846. The final line to open was that to Hastings, which was opened on 13 February 1851. The South Eastern Railway, which operated all the lines serving Ashford, merged with the London, Chatham & Dover in 1899 to form the South Eastern & Chatham, which passed to the Southern

Railway in 1923. The station as illustrated here was rebuilt in the period 1961-63. All the lines, with the exception of that to Hastings (which is still diesel operated), were electrified in the Kent Coast scheme during 1962.

Ashford Works was initially planned in February 1846 and opened the following year, replacing the earlier site at New Cross Gate. The works were extended in 1850 when carriage and wagons works were also established. Ashford built locomotives for both the SER and for the SECR, although its role diminished after the Grouping. It continued to build locomotives, including the three SR diesel shunters of 1937, through World War 2 (when it constructed locomotives to Stanier's designs as well as Bulleid's 'Q1' 0-6-0s) and beyond. The locomotive works closed in 1962, but the wagon works continued, whilst EMU maintenance was introduced to a new facility, Chart Leacon (situated slightly to the west of this view along the Tonbridge line), which was opened in 1961.

The scene at Ashford today is radically different. The station has been rebuilt to handle Eurostar services linking London with Paris and Brussels and to accommodate these services a third island platform has been constructed (platforms Nos 5/6). International trains use the middle of the three island platforms (Nos 3/4), and a new international station has been constructed on the southside; the new station opened on 6 September 1996 for domestic services. In connection with the rebuilding, the 1961-63 station buildings have been swept away and replaced by a new concourse. Elsewhere, Ashford retains its connections to Maidstone, Canterbury and the rest of Kent, as well as the main line from Tonbridge to Folkestone (over which the Eurostar services operate). Chart Leacon Works survives (although now owned by Chart Leacon Rail Maintenance Ltd) but the wagon works has closed; there remains a certain amount of activity on the latter site, however. West Yard is also still active as are the down carriage sidings alongside the Canterbury line. **(SV4195/674569)**

AYLESBURY

Then: 13 April 1964
Now: 15 August 1997

The section of line through Aylesbury, in Buckinghamshire, from South Junction to North Junction was under the control of a joint committee formed of two other joint committees (the Met & GC Joint — which controlled the line from Aylesbury south towards Amersham — and the GW & GC Joint — which controlled the line from Amersham to Princes Risborough). The line north of Aylesbury towards Quainton Road was controlled by the Met & GC Joint. There was also an ex-LNWR branch to the town, but the terminus (High Street) serving this line was to the east of the view shown here (and closed to passengers on 2 February 1953 and to freight on

2 December 1963). The first railway to serve the town was, in fact, the ex-LNWR line from Cheddington, which opened on 10 June 1839. The branch from Princes Risborough opened on 1 October 1863; this was the route by which the GWR reached the town. The line north, towards Verney Junction, was opened by the Aylesbury & Buckingham Railway on 23 September 1868; initially operated by the GWR the route was taken over by the Metropolitan Railway in 1891. The Metropolitan main line from the south opened on 1 September 1892. The importance of the town in railway terms grew dramatically with the opening of the Great Central's London Extension in 1898 (freight) and 9 March 1899 (passengers). Following formation of the London Passenger Transport Board in 1933, Metropolitan services ceased to operate north of Amersham on 9 September 1961.

As can be seen, the station at Aylesbury, which dates to c1890, is largely unchanged. The sidings east of the station have, however, been converted to a car park and the sidings north of the station have been completely removed. These losses have been balanced by the construction of a new depot for the maintenance of the Chiltern Line DMUs. Passenger services continue to serve Aylesbury both over the ex-Metropolitan line and over the branch from Princes Risborough. Passenger services north of Aylesbury, however, over the line towards Quainton Road ceased on 5 September 1966 with the withdrawal of through services over the Great Central main line (passenger services over the ex-Metropolitan routes to Brill and Verney Junction having been withdrawn earlier). The line remains for freight traffic north of Aylesbury. **(A125196/670456)**

BATH

Then: 12 June 1964
Now: 17 November 1997

The city of Bath was served by three railway companies: the Great Western's main line from Swindon to Bristol, the Midland line from Bristol and the Somerset & Dorset Joint Railway's line from Bournemouth. The GWR line through the city was constructed as part of Brunel's broad gauge main line and opened from Bristol to Bath on 31 August 1840 and from Chippenham to Bath on 30 June 1841. The former Great Western station can be seen on the extreme left of the 'Then' photograph. The Midland Railway reached Bath with passenger services on 4 August 1869 and with freight on the following 1 September. Initially served by a temporary service, the MR's new station opened in 1870; it became known as Bath Green Park in 1951. In the distance the ex-MR line can be seen heading towards Bristol. The Somerset & Dorset Joint line on 20 July 1874. The ex-S&DJR line can

be seen coming from the south at Bath Junction.

Today, although the ex-GWR route remains operational, with InterCity 125s now run by a reborn Great Western, the presence of the Midland and Somerset & Dorset has almost completely disappeared with the exception of Green Park station itself which, after some uncertainty, has been tastefully incorporated into a new Sainsbury's supermarket. Passenger services were withdrawn from both the ex-MR and ex-S&DJR lines on 7 March 1966 and at the same time the section of line south from the Bath Coop coal siding to Writhington colliery (the S&DJR route) was closed completely, as was the section from Bath Midland Road Bridge into Bath Green Park. The section from Bath Junction to the Bath Coop siding closed completely on 30 January 1967 and the final stretch of the Midland route — from Yate to Bath Midland Road Bridge — succumbed on 31 May 1971 (although a section of this route now forms the preserved Avon Valley Railway). **(A131222/672852)**

BEDFORD

Then: 15 May 1964
Now: 16 August 1997

Served by both the Midland and London & North Western railways, Bedford possessed a complex network of lines. Visible in the 'Then' photograph is Bedford Midland Road station (1), the ex-MR station, and the ex-LNWR station, St Johns (2). The ex-LNWR line can be seen heading eastwards towards Sandy and Cambridge (3) and westwards towards Bletchley and Oxford (4), whilst the ex-Midland main line runs towards London (5) southwards and towards Wellingborough northward (6). The original MR route towards Hitchin heads southeastwards (7), whilst the ex-LNWR goods yard (with connection to the MR route) can be seen in the centre (8). Also discernible is the triangular junction that linked the connection and LNWR goods yard into the Oxford-Cambridge line (9).

The first railway to serve Bedford was the Bedford Railway, which opened between the town and Bletchley on 17 November 1846; the section from Bedford to Cambridge (incorporating the earlier Sandy & Potton) opened on 7 July 1862. The Midland Railway line through Bedford to Hitchin opened on 8 May 1857, having opened earlier in the year to freight. The MR's station did not actually open, however, until 1859 as the company originally wanted a joint station with the LNWR. This ideal was not to be achieved for some 130 years! The Bedford-Hitchin section was reduced in importance with the opening of the MR's London extension in 1868.

By the date of the 'Then' photograph, services over the Bedford-Hitchin line had already been withdrawn

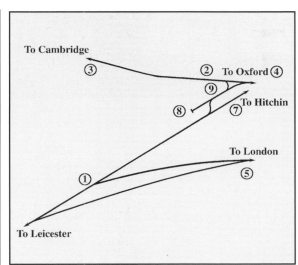

(on 1 January 1962) and over the past 33 years the town has witnessed further contractions. Passenger services between Bedford St Johns and Cambridge were withdrawn on 1 January 1968 (at which time the line beyond Goldington power station closed completely); however, those between Bedford and Bletchley, despite being threatened, have survived and now serve Midland Road rather than St Johns, running via the former link line. Services were transferred from St Johns on 14 May 1984. The last section of the former Hitchin line, the link from Bedford to Cardington, was closed completely on 28 April 1969. The line from St Johns to Goldington power station was closed completely on 6 April 1981. On a more positive note, however, the suburban services to London were electrified, the service being launched in 1983 (after a delay caused by an industrial dispute arising from proposed Driver Only Operation). The carriage sidings for the EMUs are visible in the area between the ex-MR main line and the link line to the former LNWR route. (A129196/670359)

BICESTER

Then: 10 August 1929
Now: 10 October 1997

This is one of two stations to serve the Oxfordshire town. It is situated on the ex-Great Western line from Ashendon to Aynho. The other station, Bicester Town, serves the reopened route from Oxford on the former London & North Western line. The cut-off line from Ashendon to Aynho was authorised in 1905. The route opened to freight services on 4 April 1910 and to passenger services on 1 July the same year. From the start it was used by GWR express services heading between London and Birmingham. The 'Then' photograph shows the station only 19 years after it was completed. It is interesting to compare its location amidst open fields with the considerable urbanisation evident in the 'Now' shot. The station was provided with two platform faces as well as two through roads and a goods yard.

The ex-GWR cut-off route was destined to become of great importance in the 1960s when the 'Midland Pullman' service from London Paddington to Birmingham operated over the route. However, with the completion of the West Coast electrification scheme the ex-GWR main line lost much of its importance with main line services ceasing in 1967. There was, for a time, a threat that the line would close, but it survived and in today's privatised railway the new operators (Chiltern Railways) are now operating through to Birmingham (Snow Hill) and there is investment going into the line to increase capacity. The station buildings survive, although the signalbox has disappeared, as have the through roads, and the footbridge has been altered. The goods yard has disappeared to be replaced by the ubiquitous car park. (**28273/672196**)

BIRKENHEAD

Then: 11 May 1950
Now: 7 August 1997

Situated on the west side of the Mersey estuary, Birkenhead has always tended to be slightly overshadowed by its neighbour across the river. This view, however, shows the considerable extent of both dock and railway facilities serving the town in the immediate postwar years. At the top of the photograph can be seen Birkenhead Woodside station (1), which was jointly served by the Great Western and London & North Western railways. Woodside was served by a 40 chain tunnel which started immediately after Town station (2). Also visible at this point is the entry to the Mersey road tunnel (3). Heading northwestwards from Town station is the ex-GWR/LNWR joint line to serve Birkenhead docks via Brook Street Junction (4); the docks were as follows: Great Float East (opened 1860; 5); Wallasey Dock (6); Egerton Dock (opened April 1847; 7); and Morpeth Dock (opened April 1847; 8). As can be seen, the railway

serving the docks was extensive and the amount of freight traffic then being generated was enormous. In the bottom left of the photograph can be seen Birkenhead Central station of the Mersey Railway (9); immediately after the station the line disappeared into the tunnel which passed under the River Mersey and which gave access to Liverpool.

The first railway to serve Birkenhead was the Chester & Birkenhead, which opened on 23 September 1840; this line eventually became part of the Birkenhead Railway, an operation which was taken over jointly by the GWR and LNWR on 20 November 1860. The first branch to serve the docks opened on 5 April 1847. Woodside station was opened on 31 March 1878, replacing an earlier terminus at Monks Ferry; the latter station continued to be served by trains gaining access to a coaling wharf and permanent way depot. The Mersey Railway route from James Street

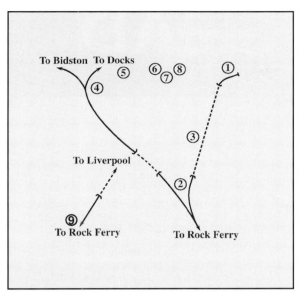

(Liverpool) to Green Lane was officially opened on 20 January 1886 by the Prince of Wales; public services commenced on 1 February. The route was an early pioneer of electric traction, being converted to electric operation on 3 May 1903.

In the space of 50 years, the changes here have been dramatic. Although Central continues to see electric services across the Mersey, Woodside station and the ex-joint line to Rock Ferry lost its passenger services on 5 November 1967. The station at Woodside was subsequently demolished. The docks remain, although as is clearly evident here, traffic is much reduced. The freight-only line to Monks Ferry closed on 20 July 1963 and that from Brook Street Junction to Morpeth Docks on 17 October 1973. Much of the dock's complex remains rail served, although access is now only from the north and the ex-joint line is now disused (traffic over the route ceased in the early 1990s). In contrast to the contraction of the railways, the local road network has considerably expanded and the entrance to the Mersey Tunnel has seen a massive growth. (A29288/670580)

BIRMINGHAM
(NEW STREET)

Then: 5 June 1933
Now: 20 November 1997

Birmingham New Street was the joint London & North Western/Midland station serving the city. The 'Then' view shows clearly the Midland side and the North Western side, although by the date of this photograph the station was controlled by the LMSR. Separating the two halves of the station is the cab road, whilst visible on the surrounding streets are a number of Birmingham

Corporation's 3ft 6in gauge trams (the last of which were to disappear in 1953). The station was first known as New Street in LNWR timetables from November 1852 and was officially opened in June 1854. At the time of the station's construction, the 212ft span of the North Western train shed was the largest such structure in the world; construction was handled by Fox Henderson & Co (a

company which also had the famous Crystal Palace in London to its name); the overall roof over the LNWR section of the station was removed in 1946 and replaced with platform awnings. At the western end of the station, the lines can be seen passing under Worcester Street before heading towards Worcester (Midland) or Wolverhampton (LNWR).

Although there are some recognisable features in the 'Now' shot — in particular a number of the surrounding buildings, such as the colonnaded Town Hall — central Birmingham has undergone a radical transformation. New Street station still survives, although the old train sheds have been replaced by an overhead shopping centre. Work started on the reconstruction of the station in late 1963. The first electric trains to operate through the new station did so on 5 December 1966 and the largely completed station was opened the following year. **(41475/672920)**

BIRMINGHAM
(SNOW HILL)

Then: 5 June 1933
Now: 20 November 1997

Snow Hill was the major Great Western station serving Birmingham; situated on the main line through to Wolverhampton, Shrewsbury and the northwest, it saw both express and local services. The first station on the site was opened on 1 October 1852 becoming known as 'Snow Hill' in February 1858. The station illustrated in the 'Then' photograph was the third station on the site and dated from a major rebuilding prior to World War 1. The north end of the station layout was remodelled in 1909 and the work, including the new roof, was completed during 1912. The new station was provided with four through platforms and two through roads without

platforms as well as four bays serving lines to the north. The classical facade making an imposing presence on Great Charles Street was the Great Western Hotel. The original hotel postdated the opening of the first station on the site, being opened in January 1868. The first hotel was, however, to prove inadequate and it was extended in 1870 to the design of Julius Chatwin. Although there were plans to rebuild the hotel in the late 1930s, these came to nothing with the onset of World War 2.

Snow Hill was destined to become a victim of the electrification of the West Coast main line, although the conversion of the latter route to 25kV saw the ex-GWR main line have a considerable swan-song. However, once the electrification process was complete and the new New Street opened, it was possible to divert all main line services away from Snow Hill. Main line services were withdrawn in March 1967, leaving only the local services northwards towards Wolverhampton and south towards Leamington Spa. The latter services were transferred to New Street or Moor Street on 4 March 1968 when the line south through Snow Hill Tunnel was closed. Although demolition work on the old Great Western Hotel started in 1969, the actual final closure of the station did not come until 4 March 1972. The old station remained until 1977 when demolition commenced. Ironically, however, this was not to be the end of the story as services were re-extended through Snow Hill tunnel to a new Snow Hill station in September 1987. Further development saw the reopening of the line north to Stourbridge Junction on 25 September 1995 and, with the construction of the new Midland Metro, services will also run from the new Snow Hill over the ex-GWR main line to Wolverhampton once again. The new four-platform station is visible in the 'Now' photograph with the track stretching northwards. Much of the local environment has, however, dramatically changed over the past 60 years. (A70921/672912)

BISHOP AUCKLAND

Then: 2 April 1964
Now: 23 October 1997

Viewed looking eastwards, the railway network of this small County Durham town is clearly evident. The station is provided with platforms on the route towards Durham (1) and a single platform (2), with overall roof (adjacent to which is a DMU), on the line westwards towards Crook (3). The main line heads eastwards towards Shildon and Darlington. In the distance can be seen the lines heading southwards to West Auckland, eventually Barnard Castle and northwards to Spennymoor. The first railway to operate into Bishop Auckland was an extension of the Stockton & Darlington, which opened from Shildon through to Crook on 8 November 1843. The North Eastern line from Durham arrived on 1 April 1857; this line served its own station until the triangular junction with the S&D route and the new station were opened on 2 December 1867. The line linking Bishop Auckland with Barnard Castle opened on 1 August 1863 whilst the final link, that towards Spennymoor, was opened on 1 December 1885.

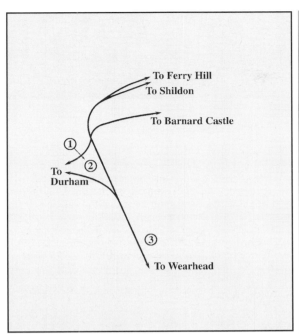

By the date of the 'Then' photograph there had already been some rationalisation — but nothing as dramatic as that to follow — with the closure to passenger services of the line to Spennymoor on 4 December 1939, that to Wearhead on 29 June 1953 and that to Bishop Auckland on 12 June 1962.

Today, Bishop Auckland is but a shadow of its former self in railway terms. Facilities have been reduced to a single platform, built in 1986, whilst the mothballed line towards Eastgate heads westwards; there are plans for the preservation of this line. The site of the former station has been cleared and redeveloped as a shopping complex. The inexorable decline in Bishop Auckland's railways continued within days of the date of the 'Then' photograph. On 4 May 1964 passenger services were withdrawn over the line towards Durham; this route was to be closed completely on 5 August 1968. This closure was followed by the withdrawal of the final passenger services west of Bishop Auckland — to Crook — on 8 March 1965. The rump of the Barnard Castle route — to Fielden Bridge — was closed completely on 12 April 1965 whilst the route via Spennymoor to Coxhoe Junction followed on 2 May 1966.
(A124905/672630)

BLACKPOOL

Then: 10 October 1952
Now: 8 August 1997

Although it was early October when the 'Then' photograph was taken, the famous Blackpool front is massed with trippers as is the beach. The crowds have, presumably, come to the seaside to see the town's famous illuminations. For us, however, the primary interest is the impressive railway terminus, which is located just to the south of that other famous symbol of Blackpool, the Tower (opened in 1894). The line to Blackpool Central, which was eventually to be controlled by the Lancashire & Yorkshire and London & North Western railways jointly, was opened between Lytham and Blackpool on 6 April 1863; it was not until 1874 that this line was linked to the earlier Preston & Wyre Railway at Lytham. The station became known as Blackpool Central in June 1878. During the latter half of the 19th century Blackpool experienced both a rapid population growth and a boom

in the number of holiday makers who chose to spend their time in the town. The station at Central was considerably enlarged in 1900 when the station illustrated here, with its 14 platforms, was constructed; the facade used brick and terracotta. In 1903 a cut-off route from Kirkham to South Shore was opened; this route was particularly busy during the summer months.

Today, the famous tower still stands, having recently celebrated its centenary, and the electric tramways — the first to operate in Britain (dating from 1885) — continue to ply along the promenade. Of Central station, however,

there is now no trace. The direct route from South Shore to Kirkham lost its passenger services on 6 September 1965 although excursion trains continued to use the line until 13 February 1967. The section of line from Blackpool Central to Blackpool South (a station renamed from Waterloo Road in 1932) saw passenger services withdrawn on 2 November 1964 and the site sold. The gas-holder remains, whilst the route of the railway has been converted, in part, to a new road and car parks. **(A47419/670551)**

BLAYDON

Then: 12 October 1961
Now: 23 October 1997

Located on the south bank of the River Tyne to the west of Newcastle and across the river from Scotswood, Blaydon possessed, as is evident here, a complex network of lines. Scotswood station (1; closed 1 May 1967) straddles the line from Newcastle to Wylam along the north bank of the river. The line heads eastwards towards Elswick and Newcastle (2) and west towards North Wylam (3). From Scotswood station the line crosses the River Tyne towards Blaydon. Immediately after the bridge, there was a junction (4) with a line heading due south (5), over the Gateshead-Blaydon line (6), towards Consett and a second route heading southwestwards (7) towards Blaydon. Looking along the south bank of the river, it is possible to see two junctions: the first (8) is a link between the Scotswood-Consett line and the Gateshead-Blaydon route whilst the second (9) allowed access to the Consett line southbound. Beyond these

junctions the line stretches on towards the staithes at Derwenthaugh (11), served by another connection from the Consett route (12), and the short freight-only branch to Swalwell (13). Finally, the junction on the approaches to Dunston can be seen (14) with one line heading inland (towards King Edwards Bridge West Junction) and the second towards the south bank of the river past Dunston staithes (and on to Redheugh).

Today, the scene is radically different. Although the Scotswood railway bridge — an 1868 rebuild of an earlier wooden structure that was destroyed by fire — is still standing, it is now devoid of track. All the railway routes previously visible on the north bank of the Tyne have disappeared. Passenger services from Scotswood towards Blackhill were withdrawn on 1 February 1954; these were followed by the closure of Scotswood station itself on 1 May 1967 and by the line from Scotswood Junction

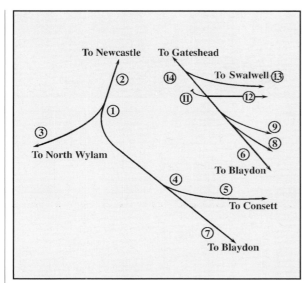

along the north bank of the Tyne, to Prudhoe on 11 March 1968. Also on 11 March 1968 the line between Newburn and Prudhoe was closed completely; the section between Scotswood and Newburn remained open until 1 December 1986 to serve the power station at Stella North. Although Scotswood station was closed, passenger services continued to pass through the site and over the bridge on services between Newcastle and Carlisle; however, these were diverted back over the original route of the Newcastle & Carlisle Railway (it opened from Hexham to Blaydon on 9 March 1835 and thence to a terminus at Redheugh in Gateshead on 1 March 1837) on 4 October 1982. The intricate network of lines that once served the north Durham coalfield have also disappeared; the lines featured here heading southwards towards Consett closing completely on 11 November 1963. Today, apart from the bridge, the only railway line to survive is the route from Carlisle towards Newcastle on the south bank of the Tyne and there is now little evidence of the enormous impact that railways and coal had on the region.
(A96899/672584)

BLETCHLEY

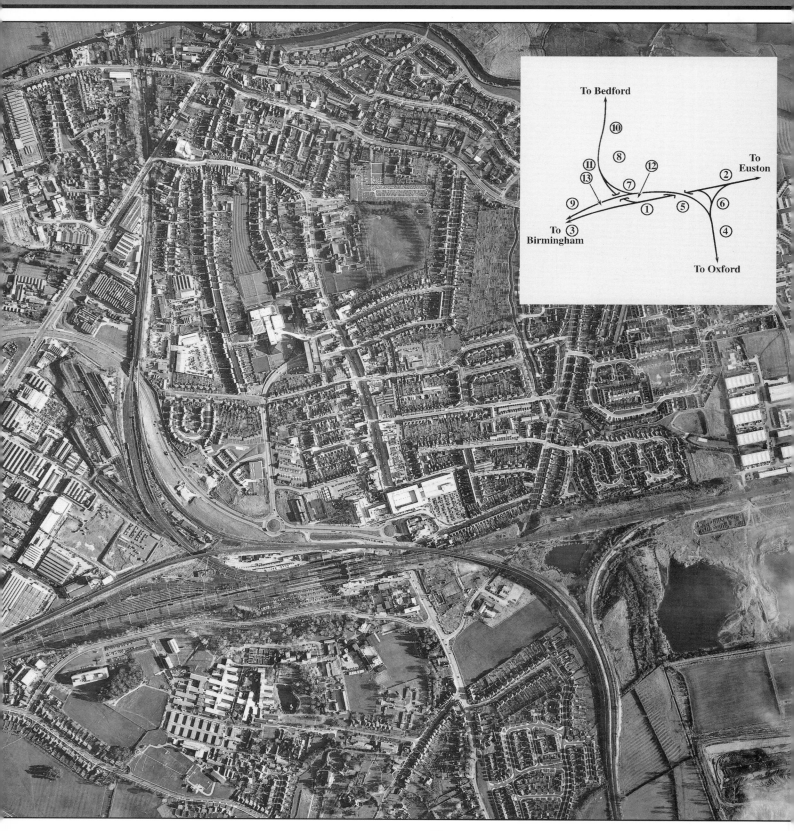

To Bedford

To Euston

To Birmingham

To Oxford

Then: 13 July 1974
Now: 4 September 1997

Whilst the majority of photographs in this book are oblique angle views, a number of vertical, map-like, views have also been incorporated. This view shows the important West Coast main line junction of Bletchley in the period immediately after the electrification of the West Coast main line. Visible are Bletchley station itself (1), with the WCML heading south towards Euston (2) and north towards Birmingham (3). The line from Oxford can be seen arriving from the west (4) before passing over the Bletchley flyover (5). The alignment from the Oxford line into Bletchley (over which passenger services were withdrawn on 1 January 1968) can be seen as can the link from the Oxford route to the southbound WCML (6). The line over the viaduct splits at Bletchley Junction (7), with lines heading east to meet the passenger line from Bletchley to Bedford at Fenny Stratford Flyover Junction (8) and north to meet the WCML at Denbigh Hall South Junction (9). Alongside the passenger line from Bedford into Bletchley (10) is Bletchley depot (11), whilst alongside the station are freight sidings (12). Further north are carriage sidings (13).

Bletchley arrived on the railway map with the opening of the London & Birmingham Railway, which opened to Denbigh Hall — the name of a pub rather than a country house — just to the north of Bletchley on 9 April 1838 and thence northwards in the following September. The line to Bedford followed on 17 November 1846 and that to Oxford on 20 May 1851. Bletchley station was rebuilt in the 1880s, but that illustrated here was the result of a further rebuilding, this time in connection with the electrification of the WCML. The flyover was the result of a policy outlined in the Modernisation Plan of 1955 for an improved freight route between South Wales and East Anglia; work started on the £1.6 million scheme in September 1958 and it was opened in 1962.

A generation on from the bold plans envisaged in the mid-1950s, Bletchley flyover remains, but it is currently mothballed and the junction with the WCML has been severed. The rusting rails heading southwards are a monument to the grand schemes (or follies?) of the Modernisation era. The Bedford line retains its passenger services, although these were under threat for many years. At the time of writing, these services continue to be operated by the so-called 'Heritage' DMU sets of North London Railways. Alongside the passenger station, freight is received in the adjacent stone termini and Bletchley remains an important station for WCML traffic despite the proximity of Milton Keynes Central. The diesel depot remains operational. **(SV5754/671589)**

BOSTON

Then: 27 August 1954
Now: 4 September 1997

This superb view of Boston in Lincolnshire shows the station and its immediate environs before the major rationalisation of the post-Beeching years. The town was a major junction on the Great Northern Railway with lines radiating northwards to Lincoln (opened 17 October 1848) and to Louth (opened 1 October 1848), southwards to Spalding (opened 17 October 1848) and westwards to Sleaford (opened 13 April 1859). The town also possessed a harbour, which was rail served and which generated a considerable amount of traffic. Clearly visible are three steam locomotives; it is unfortunately not possible to identify the types precisely, but two are clearly ex-GNR types, whilst the third, sitting in the south bay, looks as though it is a 'B1' class 4-6-0.

Evidence of the decline of the railways in the post-Beeching era is all too evident here, with the track much rationalised. The station buildings, however, remain largely intact, even if the two train sheds have disappeared. The signalbox to the north of the level crossing (West Street Junction), which dates from 1874, remains as do some of the sidings (albeit well hidden by foliage). Passenger services over the line to Lincoln were withdrawn on 17 June 1963, at which time the line was closed completely. The major rationalisation, however, came on 5 October 1970 with the withdrawal of passenger services over the line northwards from Firsby to Louth and Grimsby and from Boston south to Spalding and Peterborough. At the same time, the Boston-Spalding line was closed completely. Today, Boston sits astride the line running from Sleaford to Skegness. Although freight services had ceased to serve Boston docks, these have recently been reintroduced. **(R21517/671561)**

BRADFORD

So near and yet so far — the aerial view of central Bradford shows clearly how close the two termini — Exchange, in the foreground, and Forster Square, in the background —, were. In one of the great 'if onlys' of British railway history — if the completion of the Midland Railway's scheme for a through line through Cleckheaton had not been abandoned as a result of the outbreak of World War 1 — Bradford would have been provided with a through station. The failure to construct a central station in the city — and there were plans as late as the 1980s for such a construction — effectively consigned the city to being served by no more than secondary services.

Exchange station, in the foreground, was owned by the Lancashire & Yorkshire and Great Northern railways; each of the companies had five platforms, those of the LYR to the west, under one trainshed and those of the GNR to the east. Exchange station was built upon the site of the original LYR Drake Street terminus which had opened

with the completion of the line from Low Moor on 9 May 1850. The GNR had opened its original terminus at Adolphus Street (not illustrated) in August 1854. GNR services were diverted into the new Exchange station — with the consequent closure of Adolphus Street to passengers (it remained as a goods shed until 1 May 1972) — on 7 January 1867. Situated between Exchange station and the ex-LYR Bridge Street goods yard is the ex-GNR Victoria Hotel, which was also opened in 1867 to a design of Lockwood & Mawson (but not taken by the GNR until 1892). The hotel was sold in 1852 and remains open.

The first railway to serve Bradford was, however, the Leeds & Bradford, which opened its line parallel to the earlier Bradford Canal along the valley from Shipley. This line opened to passenger services on 1 July 1846 and to freight on the following 7 September. The original station in Bradford, known as Market Street, was rebuilt towards the end of the 19th century — officially reopening on 2 March 1890 — at which time it became known as simply 'Bradford'; the suffix 'Forster Square' was added on 2 June 1924. The station was further rebuilt during 1953 when the overall roof was replaced with platform awnings as illustrated in this view. Alongside the station, to the west, is the Midland Hotel, which was designed by Charles Trubshaw and opened in July 1890; the hotel has one great claim to fame — it is where the noted Victorian actor Sir Henry Irving died after having collapsed on stage in the city. To the east of Forster Square station can be seen the impressive bulk of the ex-MR Valley Road goods shed.

The 'Then' photograph shows that much of the city centre in Bradford had already been redeveloped. This process has continued in the 30 years since the 'Then' photograph was taken. Passenger services were all but withdrawn from Forster Square, leaving the station to concentrate on parcels traffic. However, passenger services were reprieved and a new — now electrified at 25kV — station has been built. The site of the old Forster Square station has been swept away for redevelopment, as has the old Valley Road goods yard (closed 6 August 1984); the site was largely cleared during 1992. The original Exchange station closed on 14 January 1973 when services were transferred to the new four-platform station — now renamed Bradford Interchange — that was built as part of the new transport interchange that was opened in 1977; the bulk of the original Exchange station was demolished between 1973 and 1978, although evidence can still be found. The site was used for the city's new Crown Courts. The Bridge Street goods yard had closed on 20 October 1962; the site was cleared in the late 1960s and utilised for the bus depot (underground) and surface bus station. A reflection of the changing public transport needs is that part of the bus station has been converted into the site of new offices and the buses have been removed from the underground depot to a new garage (ironically built on the site of the former Hammerton Street depot).
(A169035/673492)

BRIGHTON

Then: April 1920
Now: 18 October 1997

This is one of the oldest 'Then' photographs in the book — the Aerofilms company only started operations in 1919 — and shows the scale of the London, Brighton & South Coast Railway's presence in the town in the immediate period before the Grouping of the railways in 1923. Visible are the passenger station (1), the line towards Hove (2), Montpelier Junction (3), the line towards Lewes (4), the locomotive works (5), the main line towards London (6), the locomotive sheds (7), the London Road viaduct (8), the carriage shed and paint shop (9), and the goods line running under the locomotive works' extension (10).

The first line to Brighton was that linking the town with Shoreham, which opened on 11 May 1840. This was followed in September 1841 by the opening of the line southwards from Haywards Heath. The line to Lewes

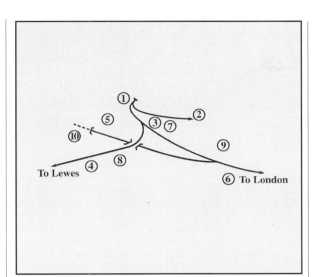

opened on 8 June 1846. The station was originally designed by David Moccatta, but was considerably modified in 1882/83 when the new roof was installed. The locomotive works dated back to the 1840s, but it was not until 1852 that the first locomotive was built, starting a tradition that was to continue for more than 100 years, culminating in the construction of BR Standards.

Today, Brighton continues to see passenger trains over the lines to Shoreham, Haywards Heath and Lewes but, as is all too visible, the locomotive works have disappeared. The site was cleared, following closure, in 1971 and now forms a carpark. Electric services were inaugurated between London and Brighton/Worthing on 1 January 1933; the old carriage shed survives as a depot for EMU stock and a number of units can be seen stabled outside it. The line to Lewes was electrified in 1935. The goods lines, which used to pass under the locomotive works, have also disappeared and the goods shed area (which was not shown clearly in the 'Then' photograph) has been redeveloped. (**683/672341**)

BRISTOL

Then: 1 November 1938
Now: 13 September 1997

This view, taken immediately prior to World War 2 and looking northeastwards, shows the approaches and environs of Bristol Temple Meads station. The station, although originally solely Great Western, had become, through the arrival of the Midland in Bristol, a joint operation and visible are lines owned both by the GWR and the MR. Dominating the foreground is the GWR goods shed (1). Alongside, between the shed and Brunel's original GWR terminus (2), are the through lines (3) that ran to Ashton Gate with a branch to Wapping Wharf. The train shed of the through station (4) with the line heading south towards Taunton. Heading away eastwards the joint line continues to GW & Midland Junction (5), where the MR main line heads towards Gloucester and Bath and the GWR line towards South Wales Union Junction (6) where the line towards South Wales heads towards Days Bridge

Junction (7) and that to Bath towards Feeder Bridge Junction (8). Also visible is the Kingsland Road goods yard (9), St Philip's Marsh locomotive shed (10) — both GWR — and the LMS (ex-MR) shed at Barrow Road (11).

The first station at Temple Meads was the Brunel designed terminus, that opened with the line to Bath on 31 August 1840. This was followed by the Bristol & Exeter, which opened on 1 June 1841 initially using Brunel's terminus (by reversing in and out). This arrangement was inconvenient, and the B&E built its own terminus at Temple Meads; the train shed of this structure was demolished when the joint station was constructed in the 1870s. The Bristol & Gloucester, forerunner to the MR, had been the first to serve Bristol, opening to a station at Avonside Wharf on 6 August 1835. It was in 1865 that powers were obtained to construct a joint

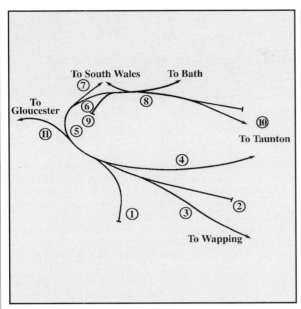

station, but work did not commence until 1871. The new station, designed largely by Sir Matthew Digby Wyatt (who had also worked at Paddington), was opened on 1 January 1878. Almost from the start the new station was inadequate, and delays became all too common. Despite this, however, it was not until after 1929 that the station was again enlarged with additional platforms. The enlarged station was completed by December 1935.

The view from the air today shows that Temple Meads station remains with its train shed, although the original Brunel terminus is no longer rail served and is being converted into a museum. The slightly altered angle allows for a view of the ex-GWR Bath Road shed immediately to the south of the station. The line from Temple Meads to Wapping Wharf closed completely on 6 October 1963, whilst passenger services over the former MR line to Yate (for Gloucester) ceased officially on 29 December 1969 (the last trains actually operated on the 27th when the line was blocked). The rump of the ex-MR line, however, survives to serve the Barton Hill wagon shops. Other disappearances include both the goods yard at Temple Meads and the Kingsland Road goods yards.
(60120/672027)

BUCKINGHAM

Then: 18 September 1964
Now: 20 October 1997

The county town of Buckinghamshire was served by the London & North Western line from Banbury (Merton Street) to Verney Junction. This line opened under the aegis of the Buckinghamshire Railway from Bletchley to Banbury on 1 May 1850 and from Verney Junction to Oxford on 20 May 1851. The latter route, forming part of the cross-country Oxford-Cambridge line was to become a major railway artery; the line through Buckingham,

however, was destined to play a very secondary role.

Closure for the line to passenger services came in two stages: the line north to Banbury closed on 2 January 1961 whilst that south to Verney Junction was withdrawn on 7 September 1964. Freight services between Buckingham and Banbury ceased on 2 December 1963, although the track was not lifted immediately as a train operated as far as Brackley in 1966. Buckingham became

isolated from the railway network on 5 December 1966 when freight was withdrawn over the line south to Verney Junction. As can be seen in the 'Now' photograph, Buckingham has expanded considerably over the past 33 years; the trackbed seems remarkably intact, however, although the station itself has disappeared (the site being used for the car park of the factory that still stands behind it). To the west the brick road underbridge still stands providing a useful reference point. (**A140779/672202**)

BURY ST EDMUNDS

Then: 13 April 1959
Now: 11 August 1997

This view looking eastwards towards the station (1) and the line onwards towards Haughley Junction (2) shows clearly the junctions at Bury St Edmunds between the Ely-Haughley line and the line towards Thetford (3) northwards and Long Melford (4) southwards, all of which were owned eventually by the Great Eastern Railway. The railway first reached Bury St Edmunds with the opening of the line from Haughley Junction, courtesy

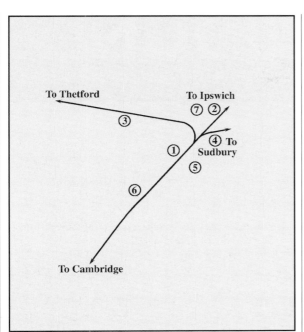

of the Ipswich & Bury Railway, to freight on 30 November 1846; passenger services followed on 24 December 1846. The line was extended westwards to Newmarket on 1 April 1854. The branch to Long Melford opened on 9 August 1865 and that to Thetford on 1 March 1876. The station, built in an attractive Jacobean style, was designed by the architect Francis Barnes, and dates from the opening of the main line. Also visible are the extensive goods facilities at the west of the station (5), the locomotive shed (6; this was classified 31E but had closed in January 1959) and the sugar works (7).

The main line through Bury St Edmunds continues to provide a vital link across East Anglia, but both the branches have closed. The Thetford branch lost its passenger services on 9 June 1953 and those to Lavenham and Long Melford ceased on 10 April 1961. Freight services over the line to Thetford were withdrawn on 27 June 1960, whilst the line south to Lavenham closed completely on 19 April 1965. As can be seen, there are now few indications of either branch. The scene is now dominated by the A14 dual carriageway. The sugar works has grown considerably over the years, but has now lost its rail connection. The station, now a listed building, survives as do some of the goods facilities on the west of the station. (**A74729/670491**)

CAMBRIDGE

Then: 3 April 1969
Now: 11 August 1997

Famous for its university but less so as a railway junction, Cambridge is nonetheless an important station on the ex-Great Eastern main line from London to King's Lynn. This view, looking northwestwards, shows the location of the railway station and goods facilities to the east of the historic centre; like Oxford, the university authorities were reluctant to see the railway close to the city's historic core, with the result that the station is situated some distance (about 1.5 miles) from the centre. Situated at the centre of the photograph is Cambridge station with its single main through platform and bays at north and south ends. In the distance the main line can be seen stretching towards Coldham Lane Junction where the main line headed northwards towards Ely and the Bury St Edmunds line headed east towards Newmarket; just to the south of Coldham Lane Junction, on the east side of the line, is the DMU depot. On the north side of the station was Cambridge shed (31A), but this had lost its steam

allocation in 1962 and had been demolished by 1969. On the east side of the main line can be seen carriage sidings and the Coalfields goods yard, whilst on the west of the main line, south of the station can be seen the ex-GNR and ex-LNWR goods yard — the latter reaching Cambridge via the route from Sandy (which had closed on 1 January 1968) — and the Brooklands Avenue oil terminal.

The railways reached Cambridge with the opening of the Eastern Counties Railway line from Bishop Stortford to Norwich on 30 July 1845. The route from Chesterton Junction to St Ives (over which the Midland eventually gained access to Cambridge) opened on 17 August 1847. The line towards Newmarket from Coldham Lane Junction opened on 9 October 1851. The GNR gained access to Cambridge on 1 April 1852 with the opening of the line to Shepreth Branch Junction (the section between Shepreth and the Junction being GER). Passenger services on the LNWR route from Bedford commenced on 7 July 1852). Other services linked Cambridge with Haverhill and, via Fordham, with Mildenhall.

Thirty years on, Cambridge has been much modernised, although the original classical station has been carefully refurbished as part of the modernisation scheme. The area was resignalled in 1981, with a new power box replacing the earlier manual structures and passenger services on the lines from King's Lynn to London and from Cambridge to Hitchin are now electrified. As can be seen the Brooklands Avenue oil terminal remains operational, as does the adjacent coal concentration yard. The Coalfields goods yard has, however, been replaced by a new Post Office sorting office and the sidings east of the station have been much rationalised. Apart from the withdrawal of services to Mildenhall (closed to passengers on 18 June 1962), to Haverhill (on 6 March 1967) and to Bedford (on 1 January 1968), only one significant closure has affected Cambridge since the 'Then' photograph was taken — the closure of the St Ives line to passenger services on 5 October 1970. This route, however, remains open for freight traffic and reopening to passenger services has been proposed on a number of occasions.
(**A198528/670507**)

CARDIFF
(GENERAL)

Then: 3 June 1933
Now: 15 August 1997

This fascinating 'Then' photograph shows Cardiff General station during the rebuilding of the station in the early 1930s. The main station is shown in the centre (1) whilst alongside are the platforms of Cardiff Riverside Junction (2), with the branch to Clarence Road (3) stretching off to the south. In the distance can be seen (4) the connection to the Taff Vale Railway at East Branch Junction (see Cardiff Queen Street over the page) with the Newtown goods yard (5) beyond.

The first station on the present site was opened with the arrival of the South Wales Railway on 18 June 1850. The station was considerably expanded during the 1890s, when Taff Vale and Rhymney services started to use the station. The Riverside branch was opened to serve the Glamorganshire Canal Co's warehouses and wharves on 14 September 1882; a passenger service from the platforms at Riverside Junction to Clarence Road was introduced on 2 April 1894. At the date of the 'Then' photograph, the GWR treated Riverside Junction as a separate station; it was not incorporated into General until 28 October 1940. The scene as illustrated shows the work in progress with the modernisation of Cardiff General. Work started on the scheme in 1931 and included the lengthening of the four existing main line platforms to 1,000ft, the rebuilding of the platforms used by trains from the ex-TVR route and the reconstruction of

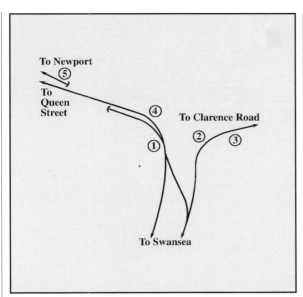

Riverside Junction station as an island platform with two 600ft platform faces. Much of this work has been completed by 1933, but construction continues on the new main station buildings; these were officially opened by Oliver Stanley MP, the then Minister of Transport, on 26 February 1934.

Today, Cardiff's main station remains largely as it was rebuilt in the 1930s. The name has, however, changed; since 7 May 1973 it has been known as 'Cardiff Central' having had the 'General' suffix since 1922. A certain amount of modernisation of the existing buildings was undertaken in the 1980s. Passenger services were withdrawn between Riverside Junction and Clarence Road on 16 March 1964, at which time the line beyond Riverside Junction was closed completely, although the platforms at Riverside Junction were retained for parcels use for a time. All traces of the Riverside Junction platforms have disappeared, although a short spur still follows the alignment. The connection to the ex-TVR route is clearer and it is also now possible to see the route of the line towards Bute Road running north to south in the background. (**41792/670401**)

CARDIFF
(QUEEN STREET)

Then: 12 May 1965
Now: 15 August 1997

This view of Cardiff taken in the mid-1960s features Cardiff Queen Street station (1) in the centre. The Taff Vale Railway line from Radyr (2) comes in from the northwest and passes through the station before heading off through East Branch Junction (3) to Cardiff Docks. The TVR split at East Branch Junction with lines running either side of the Bute West Docks; there was also a connection to the Great Western main line at this point. Coming in from the north is the Rhymney Railway (4), which ran past Adam Street goods depot (5; the RR's first passenger terminus) before heading towards Bute East. The RR originally had a station immediately north of the junction with the TVR (6), but this closed in 1928 when the GWR modified the existing junction to allow trains from Rhymney access into Queen Street station. In the foreground can be seen the ex-GWR main line with the large Newtown goods yard.

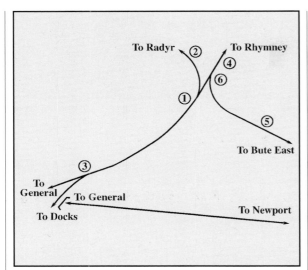

Queen Street station initially dated from 1840, but as illustrated in the 'Then' photograph was largely the product of a major rebuilding of 1887 and an expansion by the GWR in 1928 when additional platforms were provided. The Newtown depot originated in 1872 and was considerably enlarged in 1889.

The scene today shows dramatic changes. Gone are the freight depots at Newtown and Adam Street, the latter closing on 2 May 1966 (at which time the section of the former RR from Adam Street to the junction with the TVR closed completely; the line south of Adam Street into the docks had closed earlier, on 21 December 1964). Passenger services remain over the TVR route towards Radyr and over the RR route northwards. Cardiff Queen Street station was rebuilt in 1973 with a single island platform and a bay, although a further modification in 1990 saw the bay converted into a further through road. East Branch Junction has also been rationalised, although passenger services continue southwards to Cardiff Bute Road station and the link with the ex-GWR main line remains. (**A146363/670395**)

CARLISLE

Then: 24 September 1971
Now: 8 August 1997

In pre-Grouping days Carlisle could lay claim to no fewer than seven railway companies operating into Citadel station and the resulting railway network was complex. Even as late as 1971, after some rationalisation, the southern approaches to Carlisle were convoluted. Visible in this view are Citadel station (1), the remains of the Maryport & Carlisle Crown Street goods yard (2), the site of the LNWR Crown Street goods yard (closed by 1 February 1966; 3), the M&CR line heading southwestwards (4), the North Eastern Railway line eastwards (over which the Midland Railway exercised running powers; 5), Rome Street Junction (6), Forks Junction (7), Bog Junction (8), the LNWR main line heading south (9), M&CR & Joint Junction (10), the former LNWR cattle yard (11) and the LNWR route heading towards Upperby Junction from Bog Junction

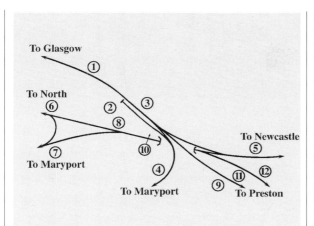

Railway. The original station was completed in 1850; since then the station has undergone considerable development, although Tite's main building has largely survived. Major work was undertaken between 1878 and 1880, at which time the overall roof was installed. When originally built, the overall roof covered an area of almost six acres, although this was cut-back at both ends in 1956/57 and new end screens installed.

The West Coast main line through Carlisle was electrified in 1974; the full service through to Glasgow was inaugurated on 6 May 1974, although some services had been electric hauled prior to that date. Citadel station remains largely unchanged although trackwork has been rationalised. Elsewhere the ex-NER line remains as does the ex-M&CR line to the Cumbrian Coast; much of the avoiding line, however, has disappeared with only the section from London Road Junction/Upperby Junction via Bog Junction to Currock Junction on the line towards Maryport surviving as a freight only route. The rest of the triangle at Bog Junction and the course of the closed route is, however, still clearly identifiable. The remaining two sides of the triangle and the avoiding line northwards were closed completely on 15 January 1986. **(A218126/670590)**

(by which route LNWR trains could avoid Citadel station; 12).

Work started on the future Citadel station in October 1845, with buildings designed by (Sir) William Tite, who had also designed stations for the London & Southampton

CARMARTHEN

Then: 26 September 1961
Now: 13 September 1997

Visible on the extreme left is the ex-Great Western Railway station serving this Welsh town. This was, in fact, the second station to serve Carmarthen as the broad gauge South Wales Railway first opened a station on what is now the main line westwards on 11 October 1852. The Carmarthen & Cardigan Railway opened northwards as far as Conwil on 1 July 1860. The route northwards eventually reached as far as Aberystwyth with branches serving Newcastle Emlyn and Aberayron; there was also an LNWR link across from Abergwili to the Central Wales line. In this view the extensive freight facilities provided at Carmarthen on the north bank of the River Towy are evident as is the relationship between the Town station and Carmarthen itself.

Although the road bridge crossing the river at this point is still extant, the railway bridge has gone, along with the extensive freight sidings. The station remains, although it has been much rationalised over the past 36 years. The slightly different angle allows for a view of the triangular junction which connects Carmarthen with the South Wales main line between Swansea and Fishguard. The siding visible on the east (ie left hand) side serves a cement

54

terminal. Passenger services north of Carmarthen ceased with the withdrawal of passenger services over the line to Aberystwyth; this occurred in two stages: from Aberystwyth to Strata Florida on 14 December 1964 (due to flooding) and Strata Florida to Carmarthen on 22 February 1965. Other passenger services northwards (to Aberayron, Newcastle Emlyn and over the ex-LNWR route) had ceased earlier. Freight operation continued from Carmarthen to Felin Fach/Newcastle Emlyn on 1 October 1973. The line across the river from Town station to Carmarthen Goods survived until 8 October 1983. As can be seen, the developers are hard at work on the site of the goods yard; it would appear that a new road is being constructed on the trackbed. Further north, however, there is better news of the former railway as the Gwili Railway has preserved a section and is looking to extend its line. (A96227/671358)

CHELTENHAM

Then: May 1960
Now: 16 August 1997

The spa town of Cheltenham was served by the lines of the Midland and Great Western railways. The MR line, from Birmingham to Gloucester serving Lansdown station, was to the west of the scene illustrated here. This view shows the ex-GWR terminus of St James, with the line towards Honeybourne heading northwestwards in the background. Cheltenham St James was opened on 23 October 1847. It was initially known simply as 'Cheltenham' but became

'Cheltenham St James' in May 1908 and was again renamed, this time as 'Cheltenham Spa St James', in February 1925. The station was rebuilt in the early part of the 20th century, but was then largely unaltered until 1956 when the arrivals' platform was extended by 150ft; this change can be clearly seen in the elongation of the northernmost of the two platforms. The station's importance grew in 1959 when all services from the

56

ex-Midland & South Western Junction Railway were
diverted to the station, but this line was to close in 1961.
The line from Cheltenham (Malvern Road East Junction)
to Honeybourne was completed in August 1899. This
provided the GWR with a through route from the West
Country to Birmingham via Stratford-upon-Avon.

Today the scene is radically altered. Cheltenham Spa St
James saw its passenger services withdrawn on 3 January
1966 and freight facilities withdrawn on 31 October of the
same year. Timetabled passenger services over the
Cheltenham-Honeybourne line were withdrawn on

25 March 1968, although the route remained for use by
diversions until complete closure came on 3 November
1977 following a derailment near Bishop Cleeve in
August 1976. The section of the route north of
Cheltenham Racecourse station is currently being restored
as a preserved line by the Gloucestershire-Warwickshire
Railway. At the time the 'Now' photograph was taken
much of the land formerly occupied by the erstwhile St
James station was still open; however, there are imminent
plans for the redevelopment of this prime site.
(**A80279/670388**)

CHESTER

Then: 9 October 1963
Now: 7 August 1997

The city of Chester — known as Deva to the Romans — was and is one of the most important regional centres of the northwest. Situated on the River Dee, the city was served by the Great Central, the Great Western and the London & North Western railways as well as the Cheshire Lines Committee. This view, taken in the early 1960s, shows the juxtaposition of the two passenger stations — Northgate (ex-CLC/GCR; 1) and General (ex-

GWR/LNWR [Birkenhead Joint]; 2) — the Chester & Holyhead main line heading southwestwards towards Saltney (3). Chester General station was opened on 1 August 1848 and was designed by Francis Thompson; it replaced earlier stations opened by the Chester & Birkenhead Railway (23 September 1840) and the Chester & Crewe (1 October 1840). The first section of the Chester & Holyhead, from Chester to Saltney, opened on

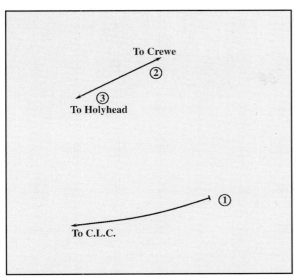

To Crewe
②

③
To Holyhead

①

To C.L.C.

4 November 1846 to allow access to Chester for trains of the Shrewsbury & Chester Railway. The CLC reached the city in the 1870s, with the line from Mouldsworth to Northgate station opening on 2 November 1874 for freight and on 1 May 1875 to passenger services. The GCR line from Chester to Hawarden Bridge opened in 1890.

Chester remains an important railway junction, although there has been considerable rationalisation. Northgate station lost its freight facilities on 5 April 1965 and passenger services were withdrawn on 6 October 1969 when the remaining services to Manchester were transferred to General via a connection at Mickle Trafford; passenger services over the ex-GC line to Hawarden Bridge were withdrawn on 9 September 1968. The station site has been converted into a leisure complex. General retains its passenger services towards Holyhead, Shrewsbury, Birkenhead Warrington and Crewe, although freight facilities have been much rationalised. There remains, however, the wagon works and a DMU depot. Services towards Birkenhead have been electrified.
(A122520/670545)

CIRENCESTER

Then: 17 May 1961
Now: 20 October 1997

The town of Cirencester was served by two railway companies: the Great Western branch from Kemble and the Midland & South Western Junction Railway. The 'Then' aerial view shows the terminus of the ex-Great Western branch. This line — from Swindon — had been opened under the aegis of the Cheltenham & Great Western Union Railway on 31 May 1841. The 4.25 miles from Kemble was relegated to the status of a branch four years later with the opening of the line from Kemble to

Standish Junction just south of Gloucester. It was incorporated into the Great Western Railway in 1843. The station was renamed 'Cirencester Town' on 1 July 1924, reflecting the GWR's acquisition of the M&SWJR at the Grouping. Visible in the photograph are the engine shed, the goods shed and the main station building. In February 1959, in an effort to improve the finances of this line and the neighbouring branch to Tetbury, the Western Region brought in lightweight four-wheel railbuses to operate the

passenger services. These, however, failed to secure the future of the line and passenger services were withdrawn on 6 April 1964. Freight facilities were withdrawn on 4 October 1965.

The changes here have been dramatic. The old road overbridge survives, but appears to have been rebuilt, whilst the old railway formation has been swept away to be replaced by the new A419(T). Elsewhere there is evidence of considerable redevelopment, although odd buildings survive from 36 years ago. One fixture, however, is the circular Roman amphitheatre located to the west of the new road.

The M&SWJR, which also served Cirencester, was located to the southeast of this area and is, therefore, out of shot. This route opened from Rushey Platt to Cirencester on 18 December and thence to Andoversford on 1 August 1891. Passenger services over the M&SWJR succumbed on 11 September 1961, when the section north of Cirencester closed completely. The section of line from Moredon to Cirencester closed completely on 31 March 1964. (**A88287/672219**)

Then: 11 October 1961
Now: 2 September 1997

Colchester, with its roots as one of Britain's most important Roman cities, was and is a major railway junction on the ex-Great Eastern main line to Ipswich and Norwich. The Eastern Counties Railway from the south had first reached Colchester on 29 March 1843, but it was not until 11 June 1846 that the route was extended, courtesy of the Eastern Union Railway, to Ipswich. The branch to the Hythe was opened on 1 April 1847 to freight. Courtesy of the Tending Hundred Railway this line was tended to Wivenhoe on 8 May 1863. The second Colchester station, St Botolphs (not illustrated but situated to the southeast of the main line station) opened on 1 March 1866. It was over the branch that the railway eventually reached Walton and Clacton. The 'Then' photograph, looking northeastwards towards the junction with the Walton/Clacton line, shows well the station as rebuilt for the electrified services and the staggered up

platform. Local services to Walton and Clacton were electrified on 13 April 1959. This scheme, upon which work had started in 1957, was the first in Britain to use the now accepted 25kV ac as standard.

Electrification between Chelmsford and Colchester was installed between 1961 and 1963, with the first services operating in March 1963. Full services were launched on 17 June 1963. The main line north of Colchester was only electrified from the early 1980s, with services between Colchester and Ipswich being electrically operated from 13 May 1985. As is evident here, the station is largely unchanged from the building constructed in the late 1950s. Goods facilities have, however, largely been displaced and a new, large, car park has been constructed to serve the station. Visible in the station are two of Great Eastern Railways' Class 323 EMUs, with additional stock stabled at the depot in the foreground. (**A96808/670680**)

COVENTRY

Then: May 1920
Now: 9 September 1997

This is one of the oldest 'Then' photographs included in this book and shows the scene around Coventry station when it was still under the control of the London & North Western Railway. Coventry was one of the stations opened by the London & Birmingham Railway when it commenced operation between Birmingham and Rugby on 9 April 1838

(passengers) and 12 November 1838 freight. A junction was created with the opening of the line to Leamington Spa, seen here heading westwards (ie to the right) at the south end of the station on 9 December 1844. This was followed by the opening of the line to Nuneaton on 12 September 1850; the junction for this line was north of the station and

thus out of view in this photograph. It was over the line to Nuneaton that, from 1 September 1865, the Midland Railway exercised running powers into Coventry, the only railway to break the LNWR's monopoly of traffic to the city. The final extension was the Coventry loop line, which ran from Humber Road Junction, further south of the station, to connect with the Nuneaton line; this opened on 10 August 1914. The LNWR station illustrated here was the result of an expansion dating from 1904.

Coventry as a city suffered devastating damage during World War 2, but remains an important junction on the West Coast main line. The line through Coventry was electrified on 6 December 1966 and the station illustrated in the 'Now' photograph was rebuilt in connection with this, being opened on 1 May 1962. One casualty of the electrification scheme was the severing of the loop line at Humber Road Junction from 10 November 1963. Passenger services between Nuneaton and Leamington Spa were withdrawn on 18 January 1965, but both routes were retained for freight and have subsequently had passenger services restored. Coventry-Leamington services were reinstated on 2 May 1977, whilst those to Nuneaton followed on 11 May 1987. In the 'Now' photograph an up Virgin Trains' West Coast main line service from Birmingham to Euston awaits departure; as usual, the locomotive is at the rear. The large goods yard which dominated the foreground in the 'Then' shot has disappeared, to be replaced by a redevelopment site and carpark, although the long footbridge has survived. **(1194/671389)**

CREWE

Then: 1 August 1953
Now: 9 August 1997

Straddling the West Coast main line and with other routes radiating out towards Manchester, Stoke-on-Trent, Shrewsbury and Chester, Crewe was one of the great creations of the railway age. This view, looking northwards, has Crewe station (1) at its centre. The line towards Manchester can be seen heading to the northeast (2), that towards Warrington to the north (3) and that to Chester to the northwest (4); all three lines converge at Crewe North Junction (5) immediately to the north of the station. To the west of the junction can be seen Crewe North shed (6); the two sheds present are those of 1868 and, closest to the main line, the Middle shed of 1865. At this time Crewe North was undergoing modernisation; to the west of the sheds can be seen the 70ft turntable built in 1950 on the site of an earlier structure; a 12-road half-roundhouse was later built, but this post-dates the period of the 'Then' photograph. To the east of the station is the

Crewe Arms Hotel (7) whilst beyond Crewe North shed is the Locomotive Works (8). To the west of the station can be seen the lines avoiding the station with Salop Goods Junction signalbox (9). The independent lines can be seen heading under Crewe North Junction to provide links with the Warrington line (at Coal Yard Junction) and with the Manchester line (at Sydney Bridge Junction).

Crewe's importance as a railway centre began with the opening of the Grand Junction Railway between Birmingham and Weaver Junction on 4 July 1837. This was followed with the opening of the line to Chester on 1 October 1840 and that to Manchester on 10 August 1842. The North Staffordshire Railway arrived from Stoke on 9 October 1848 and the final arrival was the line from Shrewsbury, which opened on 1 September 1858. The Great Western Railway gained access to Crewe over the line from Shrewsbury with the opening of its line through

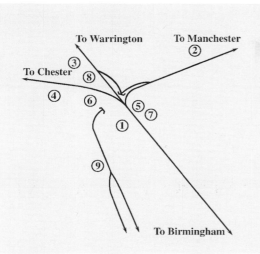

Market Drayton to Nantwich on 19 October 1863. Crewe Locomotive Works first opened in 1843 and as main locomotive and rolling stock works for the LNWR soon expanded greatly; by 1900 it employed over 8,000.

Today, Crewe remains a vitally important junction on the West Coast main line. The routes towards Chester, Warrington, Manchester, Stoke, London and Shrewsbury all still retain their passenger services and, as can be seen, the avoiding lines remain intact. The Crewe-Manchester line was electrified in 1960, with services being officially inaugurated on 12 September of that year; the line north to Liverpool saw public services commence on 1 January 1962 whilst from Crewe to Stafford the line was energised on 7 January 1963. At the time Crewe was largely unaltered — save for the introduction of catenary — but the station layout was considerably modified during mid-1985. Crewe North shed closed officially on 24 May 1965 and the site was completely closed later that year when demolition began. Apart from the carpark visible, part of the site is also occupied by the power signalbox. Crewe Works has also declined in importance, although it remains a major employer having been privatised with the rest of BREL. The part of the site adjacent to Crewe North Junction is now the home of the Crewe Heritage Centre. The slightly wider angle of the 'Now' photograph allows for a view of the junctions to the south of the station along with Crewe diesel depot (coded 'CD'), which was opened in late 1957 and eventually took over duties from the earlier steam sheds. **(R19271/670548)**

CROMER

Then: 17 August 1965
Now: 11 August 1997

Cromer Beach was one of two stations serving this Norfolk coastal town. The first railway to reach the town was the East Norfolk Railway (later Great Eastern) which opened to a station (called High from 27 September 1948) on 26 March 1877. This was followed on 16 June 1887 by the opening, under the aegis of the Eastern & Midlands Railway (later Midland & Great Northern Joint) of Cromer Beach. The GER route was linked to the M&GNR line by the construction of the Runton West/Runton East-Roughton Road line, which opened on 23 July 1906. All passenger services were concentrated at the more convenient Cromer Beach station with the closure of Cromer High on 20 September 1954.

In the mid-1960s the town was still well provided with freight traffic, as shown by the number of mineral wagons used for the delivery of domestic coal. In the bay platform

a two-car DMU awaits departure. Also visible clearly is the station building with overall roof which dated to the opening of the line in 1887.

Today, although the line retains its passenger services, freight has disappeared with a supermarket now occupying the site of the goods yard. The trackbed has been curtailed, although the original platforms are still used, and the display of 'Cromer Beach' prominent at the buffer stops 32 years ago has disappeared. The ridge and furrow overall roof has also gone, but the main station buildings are still extant. Today the station, where the trains reverse, is used by DMUs running from Norwich to Sheringham. **(A150376/670481)**

CROYDON

Then: 15 July 1951
Now: 28 July 1997

Situated in the southern suburbs of London, Croydon is served by two main stations, both of which are visible in this view looking due north. On the right hand side of the photograph is East Croydon, which serves the main line between London, Gatwick Airport and Brighton. In the top left of the photograph can be seen West Croydon, which is situated on the line from Norwood Junction to Sutton. Both these lines were operated by the London, Brighton & South Coast Railway prior to the Grouping.

Croydon can lay claim to being an early recipient of the railways, as the Surrey Iron Railway linked the town with Wandsworth as early as 26 July 1803; the line was later extended to Merstham. The extension closed in 1838 and the Surrey Iron Railway itself closed in 1846, but by that date main line railways had reached the town — the

London & Croydon opening on 1 August 1839 and the London & Brighton two years later. The East Croydon station illustrated in the 'Then' photograph is the result of the amalgamation of the earlier stations in 1897/98. Although perhaps lacking the glamour of major junctions like York and Carlisle, it is worth noting that in the early 1960s Croydon had more trains than either of these more famous locations.

Today Croydon is still a major centre for traffic on the London-Brighton main line. The station has been rebuilt as has much of the town centre. Apart from the station there are few immediately obvious reference points between the scene in 1951 and that of 1997. Commercial redevelopment has made the town one of the most prosperous in the southeast. Croydon West remains, although it is no longer as clearly visible; with the closure in May 1997 of the line towards Mitcham Junction (due for conversion as part of the Croydon Tramlink) services now operate through Croydon West on the line to Sutton. (**A68330/669423**)

DERBY

Then: 17 September 1954
Now: 16 August 1997

Derby was the home of the Midland Railway and this view looking northwards shows the station (1) being rebuilt in the early 1950s. In the foreground (2) is the London Road goods yard of the North Staffordshire and London & North Western railways. Derby South Junction (3) with the start of Chaddesden Sidings (4) can be seen at the apex of a triangular junction with Derby North Junction (5) and Derby West Junction (6) on the Derby-Duffield line. Just to the west of the main line is the Signal Works (7), which was established in 1872 and which closed in 1932. Further to the north, and almost out of frame, is the Midland Railway's St Mary's goods yard (8). Dominating the foreground, although partly obscured by the wing of the aircraft from which the photograph was taken, is the expanse of Derby locomotive works. Amongst features that can be highlighted are the old North Midland roundhouse (opened 1839; 9), the No 2

roundhouse (opened 1847; 10), the Midland Counties shed (11) and the main offices (12) linked to the station by the footbridge (13).

The first line to serve Derby was the Midland Counties line from Derby to Nottingham, which opened on 30 May 1839. This was followed by the Birmingham & Derby Railway on 5 August 1839 and the North Midland Railway to Rotherham on 11 May 1840. All these lines eventually merged to form the Midland Railway in 1844. All these three original companies built sheds/workshops at Derby laying the foundations for the future major locomotive works. It was under the MR's newly appointed Locomotive & Carriage Superintendent, Thomas Kirtley, that the works began to expand considerably, and it was under his auspices that the first of many thousands of locomotives built at Derby emerged in September 1851.

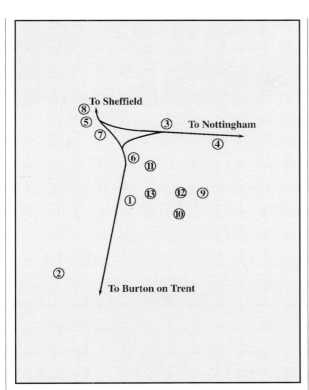

To Sheffield
⑧
⑤
⑦
③ To Nottingham
④
⑥ ⑪
① ⑬ ⑫ ⑨
⑩
②
To Burton on Trent

Close examination of the 'Then' photograph shows that work is underway on the construction of new platform awnings. This work was the result of a £200,000 scheme starting in 1952 to repair wartime damage, provide a new central footbridge and improve catering facilities. The new work was largely undertaken in concrete, providing a strange contrast with the largely unaltered design of the main station facade (by Francis Thompson) that dated to the early 1840s.

The 'Now' view provides another sorry contrast. The vast bulk of the locomotives works have disappeared, leaving the original North Midland Railway roundhouse, which is the oldest such structure in the world, marooned with odd remnants of other early buildings. The chord from Derby West Junction to Derby South Junction to serve Chaddesden Sidings remains, although the route now terminates at Chaddesden; services to Nottingham now travel over the later line to Spondon (which opened on 27 June 1867). Derby station retains the platform awnings built as a result of the 1950s modernisation, but the Thompson-designed main station buildings are no more, being demolished in the mid-1980s and replaced by a new station, the first part of which opened on 6 January 1986. The slightly wider angle allows for a view of the junction situated at the south of Derby station at which point the Spondon Curve diverges from the main Birmingham-Derby line.
(R21876/670355)

DONCASTER

Then: 21 April 1953
Now: 4 September 1997

If Derby was the home of the Midland Railway, then Doncaster was the centre of the Great Northern. The scene is dominated by two major installations — Doncaster station, which sits astride the East Coast main line, and Doncaster Works, known as 'The Plant'. Also visible, in the left foreground, are the platforms of St James' station with the ex-GCR line towards Swinton from Doncaster South Junction (which opened on 10 July 1849).

The Great Northern Railway opened to Doncaster from the north on 7 September 1848 and from Doncaster southwards to Retford on 4 September 1849. From these beginnings a major network of lines serving the district developed, as companies sought to gain access to the extensive coalfield; apart from the GNR, the Midland, the Great Central, the Hull & Barnsley, the Lancashire & Yorkshire and the North Eastern railways were all active

in the region and a complex network of lines, including numerous joint routes, resulted. The Works were, however, purely GNR. Although at the northern end of the GNR main line and there were proponents of a more central location such as Peterborough, Doncaster was selected as the site of the GNR's workshops in June 1851. Work started on the construction of the Works in March 1852 and the new Works came into operation in mid-1853. Initially, the Works handled the repair of locomotives and other work, but not locomotive construction; however, over the succeeding years the facilities were expanded and the Works built its first locomotive in 1867 — the first of many thousands culminating in Class 58 No 58050 in 1987. Carriage building started slightly earlier than locomotive building, in the late 1850s. The Works continued to expand in the last decades of the 19th century; it was at Doncaster that the first Atlantic built in Britain — GNR No 990 — was

constructed in 1898 and further famous locomotives emerged from the Plant including *Flying Scotsman* and the 'A4' Pacifics.

As can be seen, Doncaster remains both an important junction — and the slightly wider perspective in the 'Now' photograph allows for the junction with the lines to Wakefield and to Stainforth & Hatfield to be seen deviating at Marshgate Junction north of the town (along with the avoiding line which passes to the north and west) — and possessor of a major railway works. The Works are now occupied by the wagon repair business of RFS whilst the Crimpsall maintenance facility, which can now just be seen on the extreme left, is owned by Adtranz following privatisation. The station itself is largely unchanged, although East Coast main services to Leeds and York are now electrified. Note that the pedestrian footbridge, which linked the station with the Works is still extant.
(R18312C/671580)

Then: 28 April 1965
Now: 18 October 1997

Until the opening of the Channel Tunnel, Dover was the primary point of entry for rail-borne passengers arriving from the continent in Britain. This dramatic view shows the approaches to Dover Western Docks (Marine) station (1), one of the train ferry berths (2), the carriage sidings (3), Dover Town Yard (4; Town passenger station closed to passengers on 14 October 1914), Hawkesbury Street Junction (5), the site of Dover Harbour station (6; closed 10 July 1927), Harbour Tunnel (7) leading to Dover Priory station, the former Lord Warden Hotel (8; built by the SER and opened in 1863, the hotel closed in September 1939 and was converted into offices) and Archcliffe Junction (9). The first line to serve Dover was the South Eastern Railway's line from Folkestone which opened to Town station on 7 February 1844. The London, Chatham & Dover Railway's line from Canterbury to the future Priory station opened on 22 July 1861 and on 1 November 1861 these services were extended to Harbour station. By that date the original Admiralty Pier (started in 1847) had been completed and SER trains were running over it to connect with cross-channel ships. From 1861 onwards LCDR services operated over the pier as well as offering passengers a choice of two routes to London. Further development saw the construction of Dover Marine, which was opened to military traffic on 2 January 1915 and to civilian traffic after World War 1 on 18 January 1919.

With the advent of roll-on/roll-off car ferries, much of Dover's cross-Channel traffic switched to Dover Eastern Docks (off the photograph to the right). Dover Western Docks, however, remained open for rail passengers until 25 September 1994 when, with the opening of the Channel Tunnel, passenger services to the station were

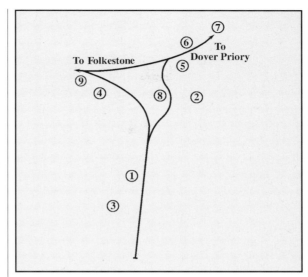

withdrawn. For a period after closure, the old station was retained as a carriage shed, but even this use has now ceased. As can be seen, the train shed still stands, but is now isolated from the main line. Some rusting sidings remain on the west side, but the complex network of lines providing access to the Archcliffe Junction-Hawkesbury Street Junction have disappeared. The owners of the building, Associated British Ports, are converting the station for use in connection with the booming cruise business. Also evident in the 'Now' photograph is one of the cross-Channel hovercraft and the fact that the area that once served the train ferry has now been infilled.
(A153491/672335)

EDGWARE

Then: 1926
Now: 1 October 1997

Edgware is the terminus of the Northern Line branch of London Underground Ltd from Camden Town. Also visible here, in the background, is the ex-Great Northern branch towards Mill Hill (which forms another branch of the Northern Line east of Mill Hill). The Underground extension from Golders Green to Edgware opened in two stages: from Golders Green to Hendon on 19 November 1923 and thence to Edgware on 18 August 1924. At the time of this photograph, therefore, the extension was less than 18 months old. There were proposals in the 1930s to construct a spur to the Edgware-Mill Hill route as part of the incorporation of the former GNR lines into the Northern Line and for the building of an extension beyond Edgware towards Bushey. These proposals, however, failed

to materialise as a result of the onset of World War 2.

The Edgware-Finchley section of the ex-GNR line closed on 11 September 1939, with the section from Mill Hill to Finchley reopening as part of the Northern Line on 18 May 1941; LNER (and later BR) freight operations continued over the whole route until 1964. The route of the proposed spur is occupied by additional carriage sidings. It is interesting to note, however, that the bridge that took the ex-GNR line over the Northern Line is still extant. Also clear is the amount of development that has taken place over the past 70 years; it is possible to see odd buildings that appear in both photographs, but the vast majority of structures have been built since the 'Then' photograph was taken. (16514/672001)

EDINBURGH

Then: 12 August 1954
Now: April 1998

The broad sweep of Edinburgh's well-known Princes Street stretches off to the east, with the famous Castle dominating the valley on the right. In the foreground can be seen the trainshed of the ex-Caledonian Railway Princes Street station, with its associated hotel forming the apex of the triangular-shaped site. On the extreme right, the ex-North British Waverley station can be seen, with the main line heading west towards Haymarket passing through Princes Street Gardens towards Haymarket Tunnels having just passed through the short Mound Tunnel, above which stands the Scottish National Gallery. Beyond the Scott Monument can be seen the huge bulk of

the North British hotel. Running along Princes Street can be seen some of Edinburgh's electric tramcars; these were to be finally withdrawn in November 1956.

The ex-NBR lines through Princes Street Gardens date back to an extension of the Edinburgh & Glasgow Railway to the new station at Waverley, which opened on 1 August 1846. Known originally as North Bridge, Waverley acquired its later suffix in the early 1850s. A relatively small station sufficed for the NBR until 1890, when the opening of the Forth Bridge brought a massive growth of traffic with the result that neither the double track section through the gardens nor the existing station could cope. Empowered by an Act of 1891, the NBR proceeded between 1892 and 1900 to quadruple the lines and also extend Waverley station; the latter was provided with a total of 19 platforms once the work was completed. The Caledonian Railway reached a temporary terminus at Princes Street on 2 May 1870, but the temporary terminus constructed there was destined to have a life of some 20 years until it was destroyed by fire. With its original terminus destroyed, the CR built the terminus illustrated here; this station, with nine platforms, was opened on 16 June 1890. The Caledonian Hotel, designed by J. M. Peddie and G. Washington Browne, was opened in 1903. The North British Hotel opened in October 1902.

Today, all passenger services in Edinburgh are concentrated at Waverley. Princes Street station closed on 6 September 1965 and was later demolished; as can be seen the station site has been redeveloped and there is no evidence that this was once a station. The hotel, however, survived and was sold in 1981. The North British Hotel was also sold and, like the Caledonian, remains in business. **(R21181/673893)**

EXETER

Then: 7 August 1973
Now: 10 October 1997

Although it is only a quarter of a century since the 'Then' photograph was taken, the most dramatic change to this scene is not to the railway infrastructure, but the construction of the canalised flood channel. In the 'Then' photograph the rail bridge for the new channel is in place. Shortly after the 'Now' photograph was taken Railtrack replaced the rail bridge over the original course of the Exe and preliminary work is already in hand at the time the 'Now' photograph was recorded.

In terms of railway infrastructure, the 'Then' shot provides a panorama of the environs of Exeter St David's station looking northwest. In the distance can be seen Cowley Bridge Junction (1), where the ex-London & South Western Railway line north to Barnstaple diverged from the Bristol & Exeter main line towards Taunton. Also visible are St David's station (2) in the centre, the diesel stabling point (3) with a number of diesel locomotives (including a Class 52 diesel-hydraulic), the goods shed (4) and goods transfer shed (5), Exeter West signalbox (6) and Exeter Middle signalbox (7), Riverside Yard (8) and the ex-LSWR line towards Exeter Central station (9).

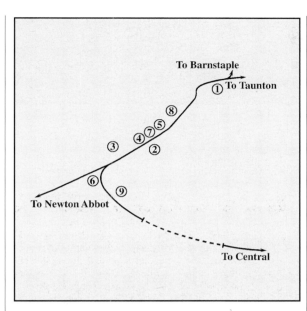

The first railway to serve Exeter was the Bristol & Exeter, which opened on 1 May 1844. This was followed on 30 May 1846 by the opening of the South Devon Railway; both the B&ER and the SDR eventually passed to the GWR. The line from Cowley Bridge Junction northwards opened under the aegis of the Exeter & Crediton Railway on 12 May 1851, whilst the last connection illustrated here, the LSWR route from Central opened on 1 February 1862. Exeter St David's station, as illustrated here, was largely the result of rebuilding immediately prior to World War 1, as modified during the late 1930s.

Twenty-five years later, there are relatively few changes to Exeter. The major difference is the result of the resignalling scheme of the mid-1980s, which saw the abolition of West and Middle boxes (and the preservation at Crewe of the former) and a certain amount of track rationalisation. Services continue to serve all the routes illustrated in the 'Then' photograph, although, as is inevitable, there is less evidence of freight. Both the goods shed and the goods transfer shed are still standing and the diesel stabling point has acquired a new two-road shed. **(269123/672176)**

FISHGAURD

Then: 26 September 1961
Now: 13 September 1997

One of the important ports serving the crossing between Britain and Ireland, today's ferries take some three hours to make the crossing to Rosslare. This is a far cry from the time that the ferries would have taken when the line to Fishguard was first opened. The South Wales Railway was authorised on 4 August 1845; this broad gauge line had, as one of its primary aims, to serve the Irish market through Fishguard. However, economic considerations arising from the Irish Famine of 1845 meant that the Fishguard route was abandoned. The first railway to reach Fishguard was an extension of the North Pembrokeshire & Fishguard Railway which opened the line to Fishguard & Goodwick station on 1 July 1899. The present day main line — from Clarbeston Road via Letterston Junction to Fishguard &

Goodwick — opened on 30 August 1906. At the same time, the short extension from Fishguard & Goodwick to Fishguard Harbour — the station illustrated here — was also opened along with the harbour. Although primarily used for services across the Irish Sea, Fishguard has also been used by transatlantic liners seeking a competitive edge on travel to London; the first to take advantage of this was the Cunard liner *Mauretania* which docked at Fishguard on 30 August 1909.

Today, little seems to have altered with the exception of track rationalisation, the virtual disappearance of freight wagons and the modification of the landward side to accommodate the inevitable road traffic. On a beautifully calm summer's day a ferry arrives past the breakwater with an incoming service from Rosslare. **(A96249/671349)**

FOLKESTONE

Then: 18 September 1950
Now: 18 October 1997

This view shows the extensive facilities that were provided at Folkestone Harbour. The Harbour branch and station can be seen in the foreground along with carriage sidings. In the background can be seen the Foord Viaduct, the construction of which delayed the arrival of the South Eastern Railway to the permanent station in Folkestone. Services from the west reached Folkestone on 28 June 1843, but terminated at a temporary station until the completion of the viaduct and the line into Folkestone

East on 18 December 1843. This line was eventually extended to Dover on 7 February 1844 and the latter seaport was soon to overtake Folkestone as the SER's primary port for continental traffic.

The harbour at Folkestone had been built by Thomas Telford in 1809, but by the time the South Eastern Railway reached Folkestone in 1843 was largely unused. The SER agreed to purchase the harbour and agreed with the Commercial Steam Packet Co to run a daily service to

Boulogne; this company was replaced in 1844 by the South Eastern & Continental Steam Packet Co, which was taken over by the SER in 1856. Work on the construction of the Harbour branch started in 1843 and the short (0.75 mile) line opened to freight traffic that same year and to passenger traffic on 1 January 1849 and the first Harbour station was completed the following year. The branch's ruling gradient is 1 in 30. Further developments saw the extension of the mole several times during the latter half of the 19th century.

The line to Folkestone Harbour remains today, although the carriage sidings have disappeared. The route was electrified as part of the Kent Coast scheme, with services commencing on 18 June 1962. The line continued to serve its primary purpose for more than 30 years after electrification, but with the opening of the Channel Tunnel in November 1994 its future is under threat. The current (1997/98) timetable shows only one working in either direction to Folkestone Harbour, running in connection with the Hoverspeed SeaCat service to Boulogne. (**R13723/672337**)

FRASERBURGH

Then: 11 June 1969
Now: 18 June 1998

The fishing port of Fraserburgh was served by a branch of the Great North of Scotland Railway. This line was authorised in 1858 and was opened in a number of stages. From Dyce, on the Aberdeen-Inverness main line, to Mintlaw, the line opened on 18 July 1861. This line was extended to Peterhead on 3 July 1862, whilst the line from Maud to Fraserburgh was opened on 24 April 1865.

This was not to be the end of the railway development at Fraserburgh, as a branch from the town to St Combs opened on 1 July 1903. This later line was, for a year from 1903, to be used by the GNoSR as one of the lines upon which steam railcars were used; the experiment proved unsuccessful and the railcars were scrapped at Inverurie in 1904.

The 'Then' photograph shows the facilities provided at Fraserburgh, including the station buildings, platforms, two-road engine shed and turntable pit, along with the freight facilities. By the date of this photograph, passenger services over both the St Combs branch — withdrawn on 3 May 1965 at which time the line was closed completely — and over the line to Fraserburgh — withdrawn on 4 October 1965 — had succumbed. There is evidence of track rationalisation and the shed, which was a subshed of Kittybrewster, and turntable have lost their track.

Fraserburgh was to survive as a freight destination until services over the line from Dyce were withdrawn on 4 October 1979, despite the booming traffic in pipelines (for the North Sea oil industry) and fertiliser; after closure this traffic was still carried, but by road from Inverurie. Today, although the fishing port remains active, all traces of the once impressive railway facilities have disappeared. As is the case so often elsewhere, the trackbed of the closed line has been converted for use as a road. **(A194524/675402)**

GLASGOW

Then: 26 July 1962
Now: 17 June 1998

With the River Clyde in the foreground, this dramatic view of central Glasgow allows us to see all four of the city's terminal stations. In the distance, to the north, can be seen the ex-Caledonian Buchanan Street (1). Further south, the familiar arched roof of the ex-North British Queen Street station (2) can be discerned. More obvious, however, are the ex-Glasgow & South Western terminus at St Enoch (3) and the second ex-Caledonian terminus Central (4). Also visible (5) is Clyde Junction on the north side of the river; it was the route through this

junction and running to the north which provided the G&SWR with its connection to the NBR at Sydney Street Junction.

The first of these stations to be opened was Queen Street, which opened with the Edinburgh & Glasgow on 21 February 1842; the station as illustrated here, however, was designed by James Carswell and constructed between 1878 and 1880. The next arrival was Buchanan Street, which was opened on 1 November 1849. This was followed by St Enoch, which was opened on 1 May 1876

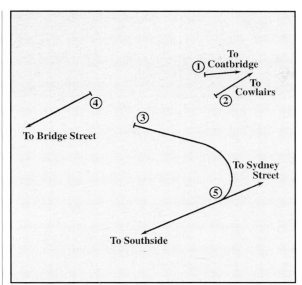

and which passed to the G&SWR seven years later. The main trainshed measured 504ft in length, 80ft in height and had a clear span of 198ft. The adjacent hotel, which opened on 3 July 1879, was at the time the largest hotel in Scotland. The last station to be completed was Central, which was designed by Sir Robert Rowland Anderson and opened on 1 August 1879.

Today, the scene is radically different. Both Buchanan Street and St Enoch stations have been closed and demolished; the former closing on 7 November 1966 and the latter on 27 June of the same year. The demolition of St Enoch in 1975, ironically the year of European Architectural Heritage, is widely seen as one of the greatest architectural losses to have occurred amongst Britain's closed stations. The St Enoch Hotel closed in 1974 and was demolished three years later. Both Central and Queen Street survive, however, although it is now impossible to see clearly the latter as it has been surrounded by more recent developments. The ex-G&SWR route across the Clyde through the remains of Sydney Street Junction also remains. **(A103483/675363)**

GLOUCESTER

Then: 7 August 1964
Now: 19 November 1997

The importance of the junction at Gloucester saw the Great Western and Midland railways construct stations serving the city. This view taken looking northeastwards shows well the juxtaposition of the two stations. Coming in from the northwest is the ex-Great Western line from Newport into Gloucester Central station (1). The ex-Midland Railway station, Eastgate (2), is located on a loop which ran parallel to the ex-GWR Cheltenham-Bristol line; the two stations are linked by a footbridge (3), which straddles the sight of the ex-MR goods yard (4). Also visible is part of Gloucester (Horton Road) shed (5); this shed (coded 85B by British Railways) was coming to the end of its life as a steam depot by this date and its last

locomotives were transferred away in December 1965. Off the photograph to the right is Tramway Junction, where the ex-MR and ex-GWR lines met; the MR lines headed towards Cheltenham whilst the GWR route headed to either Cheltenham or to Bristol.

The first railway to serve the city was the Gloucester & Cheltenham, which ran north from the Berkeley canal basin. Part of this railway was incorporated in the Birmingham & Gloucester line, which opened from Tramway Junction to Lansdown Junction (Cheltenham) on 4 November 1840. This was followed on 8 July 1844 by the Bristol & Gloucester and by the Cheltenham & Great Western Union (from Swindon) on 12 May 1845.

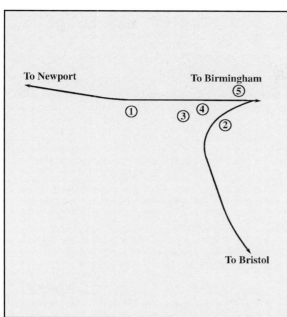

To Newport

To Birmingham

⑤

①　③④
　　　②

To Bristol

The MR took over the Birmingham & Gloucester and the Bristol & Gloucester, whilst the GWR operated the C&GWUR. The line from Gloucester towards Newport opened on 19 September 1851 whilst in 1854 the MR opened its Tuffley loop. The Eastgate station illustrated in the 'Then' photograph was the result of work undertaken in 1896.

The contemporary scene in Gloucester shows that, whilst Central station remains (albeit now known simply as 'Gloucester') all traces of the former Midland Tuffley loop have disappeared. Freight services from Tramway Junction to Hempstead goods were withdrawn on 1 August 1967 and passenger services on 6 October 1975, when all passenger services were diverted into a rebuilt — at a cost of £1.25 million — Central station. The formation of the ex-MR route survived until the early 1980s, but has subsequently been incorporated into a new dual carriageway. One result of the concentration of services is that Central station now effectively only uses one platform, since trains running from north to south or from Cheltenham to Swindon have to reverse at Gloucester. Also long gone are the goods yards and the ex-GWR Horton Road shed.
(A136132/672891)

GOOLE

Then: 27 July 1964
Now: 4 September 1997

This view, looking northeastwards, shows the ex-North Eastern Railway line heading towards the swing bridge across the River Ouse (1) with the station (2). Adjacent to the level crossing is Goole signalbox (3). Heading southwestwards comes first to Boothferry Junction (4), where the ex-NER line towards Selby diverged, followed by Potters Grange Junction (5), which was the point where the ex-NER line towards Doncaster headed southwards and the ex-Lancashire & Yorkshire Railway line headed

towards Knottingley. Access to the rail-served docks (6) was via the L&YR line. It was the ex-L&YR line to Goole which opened first, on 1 April 1848. The original impetus for the development of the port at Goole came with the arrival of the Knottingley & Goole Canal in 1825, but the coming of the L&YR, which owned its own fleet of ships, was a further stimulus to growth. The NER line from Gilberdyke through Goole to Thorne opened in 1869. The original L&YR station was situated in the dock area, but

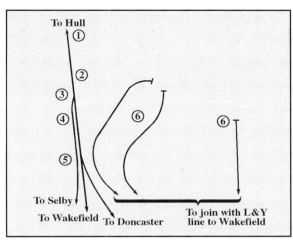

services were transferred to the new NER station on 1 October 1969. The last arrival, the line from Selby, opened in 1910, at which time the western approaches to Goole were modified so that trains arriving from the L&YR could approach either Potters Grange Junction or Boothferry Road Junction.

The Selby line was never a great success, and passenger services were withdrawn a month before the date of the 'Then' photograph, on 15 June 1964. Today, passenger services continue to operate through Goole from Doncaster to Hull over the ex-NER line and from Knottingley over the ex-L&YR route. As can be seen there has been considerable rationalisation of track, both on the main lines and in the dock area, although the latter (now Associated British Ports-owned) are still rail-served. Elsewhere, Goole signalbox still stands and the station retains its platform awnings. A westbound DMU can just be discerned in the platform. (A137005/671571)

Then: 24 October 1955
Now: 11 August 1997

This view from the south bank of Breydon Water shows the approaches to the ex-Great Eastern station of Yarmouth Vauxhall on the north bank with the Midland & Great Northern line heading over the swing bridge to form a link to the Norfolk & Suffolk Joint line towards Lowestoft. Also visible is the small shed at Yarmouth Vauxhall with its turntable; this was coded 32E at Nationalisation, although from 1957 until final closure in January 1959 it was worked as a sub-shed of Yarmouth South Town whilst still retaining its own code. Vauxhall station is off the photograph to the right. The first railway to serve Great Yarmouth was the Yarmouth & Norwich, which opened on 30 April 1844; a shorter route linking the Norwich and Yarmouth opened in 1883. The junction between the old and new routes was at Breydon Junction, slightly to the west of the area illustrated here. Other railways serving Yarmouth were the M&GN, which served Beach station (to the east) and the ex-GER line from the south which served South Town station (on the southside of the estuary). The Norfolk & Suffolk Joint line, from South Town to Lowestoft, opened on 13 July 1903, at

which time the M&GN line across Breydon Water was also opened. The bridge, designed by the M&GN's engineer William Marriott, was 800ft in length. Power for the swing span came from a gas engine with hydraulic gear. Duplicate equipment was provided because, in high winds, considerable power was required to open the span.

On the north bank of Breydon Water, trains continue to serve Yarmouth Vauxhall station over the two route from Norwich. Elsewhere, change is the order of the day. Although there is still a bridge at this point, it now serves a new road across Breydon Water rather than the railways. The ex-M&GNR line across Breydon Water was to disappear in Coronation year; passenger services were withdrawn between Yarmouth Beach and Gorleston (North) on 21 September 1953 and the line closed completely. Despite the changes, the GER box (Yarmouth Vauxhall; dating from 1884) is still extant just to the east of the bridge carrying the ex-M&GNR line over the ex-GER route. The shed and carriage sidings have, however, disappeared in favour of the symbol of the modern age — the out-of-town supermarket. (**A61747/670512**)

GRIMSBY

Then: 10 June 1969
Now: 22 October 1997

Whilst the 'Then' photograph is less than 30 years old, the transition from a railway carrying both freight and passenger traffic to one that is, at least here, primarily passenger orientated is all too obvious. The vast quantity of freight traffic, including cars (presumably for export), generated by the town's busy docks and the provision of rail facilities to the docks themselves is evident. Even in 1969, however, there are traces of gradual rationalisation; notice, for instance, the termination of the junction just to the east of the station adjacent to the new road bridge. The rapid development of Grimsby as a port took place in the 19th century, particularly after the creation of a new company in 1845. The result were the Royal Docks, opened by Prince Albert in 1849; the locks for these docks

were hydraulically operated from the 300ft high brick tower illustrated in the photographs. Grimsby was also a major fishing port, a trade encouraged by the arrival of the railways, which enabled fish to be quickly shipped inland. The section of line, constructed by the Manchester, Sheffield & Lincolnshire Railway (later GCR), from Grimsby Town station to the Docks station (illustrated here) and the network of lines serving the docks opened on 1 August 1853. The passenger line was extended through to Cleethorpes on 6 April 1863.

Today, the railway through Grimsby Docks station and on to Cleethorpes has been singled and the vast freight traffic of 30 years ago is simply a thing of the past. There is still some rail access to the Royal Docks, via the line that also serves Immingham Docks (an installation, ironically, that the Great Central Railway constructed in the years prior to World War 1 to relieve congestion at Grimsby). Fishing, too, has suffered a decline, but the boom in leisure sailing is evident with the number of yachts moored up. **(A186711/672600)**

GUILDFORD

Then: 19 September 1964
Now: 28 July 1997

Guildford station (1) is located to the west of the town centre and this view, looking north, shows the lines heading west towards Aldershot (2), north towards Woking (3) and east towards Clandon (4). Just to the south of the station is the locomotive shed (5) with its turntable. The shed was coded 70C and in 1965, shortly after this photograph was taken, still housed some 28 steam locomotives (including the now preserved Class USA 0-6-0T No 30072). The shed's coaling stage (6) was located adjacent to the station. South of the shed the running lines passed into Chalk Tunnel before heading towards Portsmouth. The first railway to serve Guildford

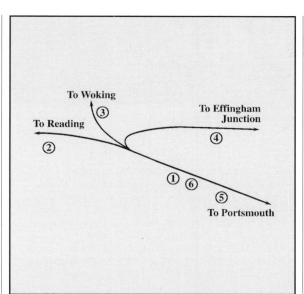

was that from Woking, which opened on 5 May 1845. The line towards Aldershot opened on 8 October 1849; the same year saw the route to Godalming opened on 15 October and the line towards Dorking on 20 August. The now-closed line from Horsham reached Guildford in 1865. The last line to open was that from Guildford towards Clandon, which opened on 2 February 1885. The station as illustrated in the 'Then' photograph was rebuilt in the 1880s and the first electric services to operate to the town did so in 1925.

In the 30 years since the 'Then' photograph was taken, Guildford's importance has increased as both a regional centre and as a residential area for commuters to London. Its status has been increased by the completion of the cathedral and by the opening of a university. Much of the city's central area has been redeveloped and the site of the former engine shed (which closed with the end of Southern Region steam in July 1967) has also been redeveloped. The lines towards Aldershot, Woking and Clandon remain open and the station itself has undergone a major rebuild, the work being completed in the early 1990s.
(A139165/669426)

HALIFAX

Then: 21 February 1950
Now: 9 March 1998

Located on the ex-Lancashire & Yorkshire line from Sowerby Bridge to Bradford, Halifax was also the junction for the Halifax & Ovenden Joint (LYR/GNR) line towards Queensbury. Halifax station is situated in the centre of this view, which is taken looking almost due north. The ex-LYR line comes in from the south and heads off to the northeast; almost immediately after leaving Halifax, the ex-LYR line heads into the 1,105yd long Beacon Hill Tunnel. The Halifax & Ovenden Joint line approaches

Halifax station over the curved viaduct from Halifax North Bridge station, which was located about a mile distant, beyond the cooling towers of the power station. Also visible are the extensive goods facilities provided by the LYR at Halifax and the impressive signalbox at the east end of the station; this dates from 1884.

The railway first reached Halifax with the opening of the Manchester & Leeds (later LYR) branch from North Dean to Halifax (Shaw Syke), which opened on 1 July

1844. The line was extended from Halifax (Shaw Syke) through the site of the station illustrated here and on to Low Moor via Beacon Hill Tunnel on 7 August 1850, at which time the original terminus as Shaw Syke closed. Halifax station has been graced by a number of suffixes: 'Old' from June 1890 and 'Town' from 30 September 1951 until the suffix was dropped on 12 June 1961. The Halifax & Ovenden line opened from Halifax to Halifax North Bridge for freight on 17 August 1874 and thence to Holmfield on 1 September 1874; the line opened for passenger traffic on 1 December 1879.

Passenger services from Halifax to Bradford and Keighley via the Halifax & Ovenden Joint line were withdrawn 23 May 1955 whilst freight beyond North Bridge succumbed on 27 June 1960. This left the rump of the Halifax & Ovenden, from Halifax to North Bridge, to carry freight until 1 April 1974, when the final section was closed. The viaduct was largely demolished in 1981.

Today, Halifax is served by DMUs operating between Bradford and Manchester or Blackpool. The station, which is listed and which has undergone some renovation work, is primarily the result of a major rebuild by the LYR in 1885. As with other major industrial centres, the decline in the level of freight traffic is noticeable. Much of the old goods yard is now occupied by the Museum of the Working Horse. It is almost impossible to determine the line of the route towards North Bridge, but many of the town's historic buildings — such as the square Piece Hall — can be clearly identified. **(A28057/673500)**

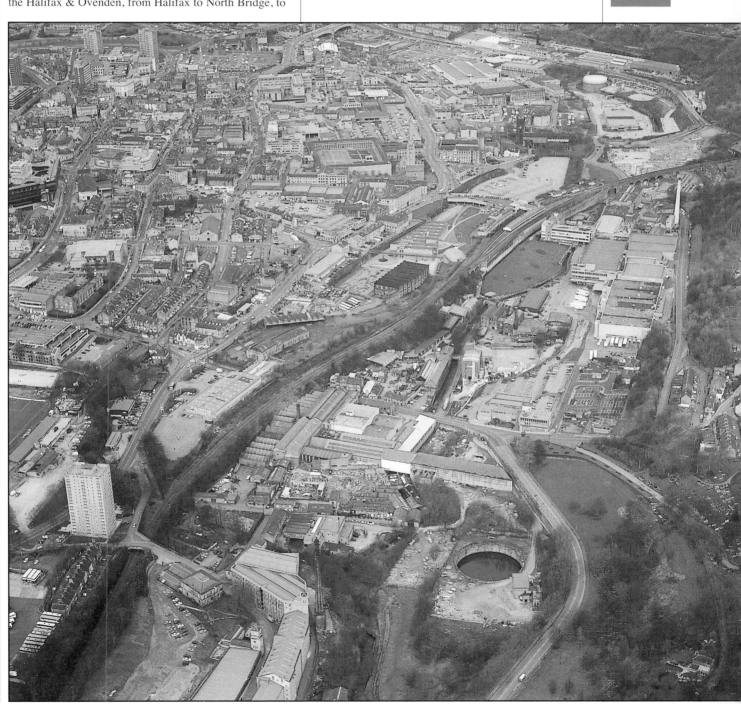

HARWICH

This dramatic photograph shows not only the railway presence in this Essex port but also the scale of the flooding that affected much of East Anglia in early 1953. The floods occurred on the evening of 31 January and were the result of a combination of high tides and gale force winds. The Harwich branch was severely disrupted. Harwich, Dovercourt and Parkeston Quay were cut-off and services were restored between Wrabness and Parkeston Quay on 5 February and it was not until 23 February that services were restored to Harwich. The bridge-ramp serving the train ferry from Harwich to Zeebrugge was damaged by the ferry *Essex* and was only restored to use on 5 March 1953. There were numerous casualties in the floods and services were disrupted over much of the east of the country. The view illustrated here, therefore, is during the period when trains were unable to reach Harwich and the train ferry service was suspended.

The railway first reached Harwich with the opening of the branch from Manningtree on 15 August 1854, but in the early years the line was not successful. It was only with the development of Great Eastern Railway operated steamers from the town after 1863 that the line's prosperity increased. Train ferries were introduced on 24 April 1924 linking the port with Zeebrugge.

Today, Harwich has reverted to being a passenger line with the section beyond Parkeston Quay (now Harwich International) being treated as a single line. Parkeston Quay, which was originally authorised in 1874, has come to dominate both passenger and freight traffic from this side of the estuary, whilst, with the opening of the Channel Tunnel, the last of the train ferry services was withdrawn in mid-1994. As can be seen, the level of facilities at Harwich has declined significantly over the past 45 years, and the link to the former train ferry berth is now no more. On a more positive note, services over the branch, operated by the modern Great Eastern, are now electric, 25kV operation being inaugurated in 1986. **(A48285/670673)**

HAYWARDS HEATH

Then: 7 August 1932
Now: 28 July 1997

Haywards Heath is one of the most important intermediate points on the ex-London Brighton & South Coast Railway route linking London with the Sussex coast. The London & Brighton Railway reached Haywards Heath on 12 July 1841 and the line was extended southwards to Brighton on the following 21 September. This view is taken looking southwards, with the line disappearing in to Haywards Heath tunnel. Just to the north of Haywards Heath was Copyhold Junction, where a line towards Horsted Keynes diverged; this route opened on 3 September 1883. Although the route diverged at Copyhold Junction, the branch junction was at Haywards Heath and it was not until 1931 that an actual connection was made at Copyhold Junction. The two-coach train is probably forming a service towards Horsted Keynes. At the time the 'Then' photograph was taken, the London-Brighton route was being electrified by the Southern Railway. Part of the electrification scheme included the rebuilding of

Haywards Heath station and evidence of the new construction work is evident here. The station was originally provided with single platform faces on the main line, with up and down bay platforms at each end; the reconstructed station was provided with two island platforms, each of 800ft in length. New station buildings were also constructed at this time. In addition, the layout of the goods yard was modified and a new goods shed was also constructed. Although electric services were tested in late 1932, the actual inauguration of through services to Brighton took place on 1 January 1933.

Today, the facilities for passengers remain largely unchanged to those provided in 1933, with two long island platforms. The major change here is, however, the disappearance of the goods yard and shed, replaced, as in so many other places, by a car park. The town of Haywards Heath has also grown dramatically over the past 60 years. Passenger services no longer travel to Horsted Keynes (despite electrification, the route was closed on 28 October 1963) although freight continues to use the line as far as Ardingly from Copyhold Junction. **(39526/669429)**

Then: 7 October 1959
Now: 12 November 1997

This view, looking northwest from the city centre towards the racecourse, shows how extensive the railway facilities were even in a relatively small location as late as 1959. Visible here are the ex-GWR Barton Street goods yard (1), the ex-Midland Railway Moorfields goods yard (2), the ex-MR line towards Hay (3), Moorfields Junction (4), Barton Curve Junction (5), Barrs Court Junction (6), the line towards Shrewsbury and Worcester (7), Brecon Curve Junction (8) and the line towards Hereford station (9).

Today, although there are odd points of reference (most

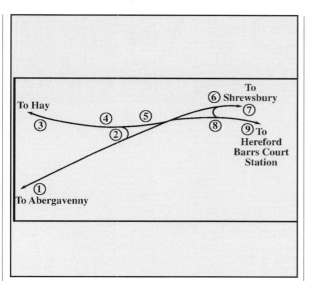

notably the racecourse and the buildings along the road in the foreground), it is difficult to comprehend that the railway was such a dominant presence. Off the 'Now' photograph to the right, the city of Hereford is still served by services on the Shrewsbury-Newport and Worcester-Hereford lines, but the complex series of lines that existed in 1959 have all but disappeared. Passenger services over the line towards Hay were withdrawn on 31 December 1962; at the same time freight beyond Eardisley was withdrawn. The section from Hereford to Eardisley closed on 28 September 1964. The section of the avoiding line from Red Hill Junction to Barton Goods closed on 1 August 1966 (the passenger service from Rotherwas Junction [Hereford], via Red Hill Junction, to Gloucester having been withdrawn on 2 November 1964) at the same time as the line from Barrs Court Junction to Moorfields Junction. Barton Goods itself closed in 1979, leaving the railway to continue to serve H. P. Bulmers cider works (at which, for a period ex-GWR 'King' No 6000 was on display) and a small number of other freight sidings. These survived until the early 1990s. (**A79098/672904**)

HOLYHEAD

Then: 6 August 1962
Now: 9 September 1997

Holyhead has, for a long period, been the primary port linking Britain with Ireland. It was Telford who rebuilt the main road to Holyhead — the modern A5 — and it was inevitable that the port would act as a magnet for railway promoters eager to capitalise on the heavy traffic and post between the two islands. For a period after 1839, due to the arrival of the railway, Liverpool supplanted Holyhead as the primary port for the Irish Mail, but this was shortlived as, on 4 July 1844, the bill authorising construction of the Chester & Holyhead Railway — except for the crossing of the Menai Strait (received the following year) — received the Royal Assent. The line opened between Chester and Bangor on 1 May 1848 and between Holyhead and Llanfair PG on the following 1 August. The section over the Britannia Bridge opened in two phases: the up line on 5 March 1850 and the down line on the following 19 October. The London & North Western took over the route in 1959. The station and railway hotel illustrated here were opened in 1880, although the hotel closed in 1951. The scale of the railway at Holyhead is apparent; at this

stage most passengers would have been on foot and freight traffic was also considerable. There was also a second — segregated — railway at Holyhead; this was used for the maintenance of the breakwater visible in the background. For a long period this was home to the two surviving Class 01 diesel shunters, but these were withdrawn in 1979 and 1981 and scrapped on site.

Today the railway still has a major presence at Holyhead, although the 1880 hotel has been demolished and replaced with a more modern structure. Elsewhere the infrastructure associated with the roll-on/roll-off ferry operation of the modern age is all too apparent. Note, in particular, the development of Salt Island in the background. **(A107156/671419)**

HULL

Then: Undated (circa early 1950s)
Now: 22 October 1997

Hull Paragon is, without doubt, one of the finest railway stations in the United Kingdom and it is only from the air that a true sense of its scale can be gained. The classical facade of the station, clearly evident in the 'Then' photograph was designed by George Townsend Andrews in 1848. The train shed was the work of a later employee of the North Eastern Railway, William Bell, and dates from 1905 when the station was enlarged. The original Paragon station took over from an earlier station constructed by the Hull & Selby Railway, which opened on 1 July 1840 and was leased by the York & North Midland on 1 July 1845. Notice the superb range of ex-LNER coaches in the station and carriage sidings; there are also at least six tank locomotives hard at work.

Hull is still an important station, although as can be seen the number of platforms in use has been reduced, leaving the northernmost two arches of the train shed no longer fulfilling a railway role. The number of sidings has also considerably declined and, in place of the six locomotives operating more than 40 years ago, Hull Paragon is apparently devoid of activity at this time. Fortunately, however, Andrews' superb classical facade remains to remind all intending passengers of the great days of Britain's railways. (**A28629/672576**)

HUNSTANTON

Then: 2 September 1959
Now: 11 August 1997

Another Norfolk coastal resort, Hunstanton was the terminus of the Lynn & Hunstanton Railway from King's Lynn. This route opened on 3 October 1862 and, amongst other aspects of its history, achieved regular royal patronage when Edward, Prince of Wales, bought Sandringham House in the same year. The royal station serving Sandringham was at Wolferton. The L&HR was to become part of the Hunstanton & West Norfolk Railway

before being absorbed by the Great Eastern Railway on 1 July 1890. As can be seen, Hunstanton was provided with extensive facilities. These included the four-platform station, carriage sidings, turntable and two-road locomotive shed (which was a sub-shed of King's Lynn [31C]), hotel and goods yard.

Today, however, the railway is long gone; unlike Sheringham and Cromer on the north Norfolk coast,

114

Hunstanton is only accessible by road. Its popularity, judging by the number of caravans and cars is undiminished. The line saw the introduction of DMU operation on 3 November 1958, but the line's finances continued to deteriorate during the 1960s, despite a number of cost savings. For example, all services were concentrated on to a single platform here on 12 February 1967. Passenger services were withdrawn between Hunstanton and King's Lynn on 5 May 1969, at which time the line was closed completely. Today the site of the station is occupied by a car park and the carriage sidings have disappeared in favour of a coach park. The track bed has been incorporated into a new road. The railway is not the only product of the Victorian age to have disappeared; the pier, which also dated from the 1860s, is another victim. **(A78516/670523)**

HUNTINGDON

Then: 10 June 1961
Now: 16 August 1997

Huntingdon was served by two lines — the Great Northern Railway's East Coast main line (situated slightly to the west of the view illustrated here) and the route from St Ives to Kettering. The second route was ex-Midland Railway from Kettering to Huntingdon and ex-Great Northern & Great Eastern Joint thence to St Ives. The section illustrated here is the ex-GN&GE route crossing the River Ouse between Huntingdon on the west bank of the river and Godmanchester (with its station) on the east. The line from

St Ives, which opened on 17 August 1847, was in fact the first railway to serve the area, reaching Godmanchester (served by a station called Huntingdon until 1 July 1882), where for a short while the line terminated. The GNR route was opened on 7 August 1850 and the line from St Ives was extended to a junction with the new route on 29 October 1851. The Midland line from Kettering opened on 21 February 1866 with a direct connection into the GER line. The early 1880s witnessed the creation of the GN&GE

Joint and the construction of a new station — which became Huntingdon East in 1923. By the date of the 'Then' photograph passenger services between Kettering and St Ives had been withdrawn (on 15 June 1959) although Huntingdon East continued to see passenger services on Fridays via the GN route until 18 September 1959.

Today, there is little to remind people that this was once the route of a cross-country railway line. Freight services along the route were largely withdrawn at the same time as the passenger services, the lines from Kimbolton to Huntingdon East and Godmanchester to St Ives closing completely on 15 June 1959. At the time of the 'Then' photograph, therefore, the only traffic was from Huntingdon North to Godmanchester and this was destined to be withdrawn on 4 April 1962. As can be seen, the railway infrastructure has been completely eliminated in favour of the new A14 trunk road. Huntingdon has also gained a ring-road and the multi-storey factory that stood behind the old station in Godmanchester has been replaced by a newer unit. (**A90629/670363**)

INVERURIE

Then: 19 October 1962
Now: 18 June 1998

Inverurie is one of Britain's forgotten railway towns. Although situated on the main Great North of Scotland Railway line from Aberdeen to Huntley, which opened on 12 September 1854, the town's primary importance as a railway centre came with the transfer of the GNoSR's locomotive workshops from Kittybrewster. The existing site at Kittybrewster was inadequate by the end of the 19th century and work started on the new works at Inverurie in late 1898. The first buildings to be occupied were those of the carriage and wagon department, which moved in 1901, whilst the locomotive works opened the following year. Finally, the permanent way department followed in 1905. In order to accommodate the staff, the GNoSR also constructed a large number of houses around the works. The station at Inverurie, which was also the junction for the branch to Old Meldrum (opened 1 July 1856; closed to passengers on 2 November 1931 and to freight on 3 January 1966), was relocated closer to the works on

118

10 February 1902 and this is the station that is illustrated here.

Although the works at Inverurie were capable of building locomotives, constructing 10 by 1921, after 1923 the locomotive works concentrated upon repair work. Illustrated here are the carriage and wagon works on the west with the paint shop nearer the camera. Between the carriage works and the locomotive works to the east is the smithy. The site passed through LNER ownership to

British Railways in 1948, being transferred to the BR Workshops Division in 1962 when many other smaller works were closed. Inverurie Works was to close completely on 31 December 1969. Today, the station survives to serve trains on the Aberdeen-Inverness route. As can be seen, although the locomotive works and paint shop have been demolished, both the carriage works and smithy survive in alternative use. **(A107856/675394)**

IPSWICH

Then: 12 June 1969
Now: 2 September 1997

Situated on the estuary of the River Orwell, Ipswich was and is an important administrative centre — the county town of Suffolk — as well as historically an important port serving the region. This latter role has declined with the growth of both Felixstowe and Harwich. This view, taken looking eastwards, shows the River Orwell stretching towards the North Sea. From the south comes the ex-Great Eastern Railway main line (1) from Colchester. As it approaches the town, it passes Halifax Junction (2), where the freight-only link to Griffin Wharf (3) joins the main line. The main line then curves towards Ipswich Tunnel (361yd long; 4), having passed the site of the original station and later locomotive depot (5) before entering

Ipswich station (6). Across the river can be seen some of the railway facilities serving the harbour area (7). With the angle that this view allows, it is also possible to see in the distance (8) the single track line towards Felixstowe.

The first railway to serve Ipswich was the Eastern Union Railway, which provided a link between Ipswich and Colchester from 15 June 1846; this served a station built to the south of the tunnel. The next arrival was the Ipswich & Bury Railway, which opened to passenger services on 24 December 1846. The main line north to Norwich from Haughley Junction opened in 1849. The original, terminus, station in Ipswich was inconvenient, as trains from the north had to reverse into it and a new

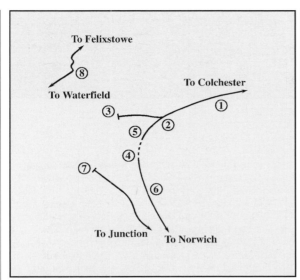

station, north of the tunnel, was opened on 1 July 1860. The station was extended, with the provision of an additional platform, in 1880.

Ipswich remains an important railway centre. Apart from the main line services from Norwich to London, branch services operate over the lines to Lowestoft, Felixstowe and Bury St Edmunds. Main line services between Ipswich and Colchester were electrified from 13 May 1985; some services northwards to Stowmarket were electrified on 22 July 1985 and full electric services to Norwich were inaugurated on 11 May 1987. The station also sees a considerable amount of freight traffic, much of it containerised from Felixstowe. As can be seen, the bridge across the River Orwell serving the dock area remains to serve the Ipswich Freight Terminal, as does the line towards Griffin Wharf, although the latter is not in regular use. The site of the former locomotive shed is still extant for C&W work having been used as a base during the 1980s for the electrification work. Notice in the background the new Orwell roadbridge carrying the main A14 towards Felixstowe. (**SV2087/670687**)

KING'S CROSS
ST PANCRAS

Then: 8 October 1964
Now: 28 July 1997

Rarely can two so dramatic but contrasting stations have been built in such proximity as at King's Cross and St Pancras. The utilitarian styling of the former forms a striking comparison with the high Victorian Gothic of the latter, whilst sandwiched between is the Great Northern Hotel. The extensive goods facilities provided are also evident with the ex-Midland Railway Somers Town goods on the extreme left and the ex-Great Northern terminal to the north. By this date, modernisation was taking full

effect and evidence of modern traction is visible outside both stations, particularly around the stabling point at King's Cross.

The Great Northern terminus was the first to open, on 14 October 1852. It was designed by Lewis Cubitt and featured two train sheds, each of 105ft in width. These were originally constructed from laminated timber ribs, but these were later replaced by iron. The Great Northern Hotel followed in 1854. The station was provided with

additional platforms, including those serving local trains, in the 1860s and 1870s. Initially, using the Bedford-Hitchin line, Midland services also served King's Cross, but the ambitious MR opened its own line through to London. The MR's extension opened for freight on 8 September 1867, for local traffic (to Moorgate) on 13 July 1868 and to St Pancras on 1 October 1868. The trainshed, with its 243ft span, was designed by W. H. Barlow and R. M. Ordish, whilst the Midland Grand Hotel was the work of the famous Victorian architect Gilbert Scott. Although built as a hotel, by the date of the 'Then' photograph it had already been converted into offices, a role it was to fulfil until the early 1980s when it entered a state of limbo.

Today, both King's Cross and St Pancras retain passenger services and these are now electric, with the exception of services from St Pancras over the Midland main line north of Bedford. Elsewhere, however, there

have been changes. The Somers Town goods yard lost its freight facilities on 5 June 1967 and closed completely on 23 April 1968 when coal traffic ceased; it has now become the site of the controversial new British Library, which opened in 1997. There has also been a considerable reduction in freight traffic to the ex-GNR yard. King's Cross has gained a new concourse, which houses ticket office and retail outlets; this opened on 3 June 1973. The Somers Town area remains between the two stations, although this and the familiar gasometers are under threat of redevelopment as part of London & Continental's controversial scheme to use St Pancras as the terminal station for the fast link to the Channel Tunnel. The Midland Grand Hotel has also seen some restoration work and is to be reconverted back into a hotel as part of the L&C scheme; some internal restoration work has been undertaken, and the interior of the building is now regularly used in television dramas. (**A143768/669445**)

Then: 14 August 1950
Now: 11 August 1997

The Norfolk port of King's Lynn was an important railway centre. Illustrated here is the main ex-Great Eastern Railway terminus in the town, with its locomotive shed and goods facilities. Heading off to the right are the lines towards the Alexandra Docks. King's Lynn was linked to the railway map on 29 October 1846 with the opening of the first 10 miles of the future main line south to Ely (it opened through on 26 October 1847). The local network soon expanded with the opening of the line to Narborough in 1846, the Harbour branch (situated slightly to the south of the area illustrated here), the Hunstanton branch (on 3 October 1862) and the Alexandra Docks branch (on 10 June 1870). Although not illustrated, King's Lynn was also served by the Midland & Great Northern Joint Railway.

Over the past 50 years, there have been changes at King's Lynn, although this location is still recognisable.

The station has seen the introduction of electric services (on 22 August 1992) and a four-car Class **EMU** can be seen. The Alexandra Docks branch remains, although the once busy freight facilities are now much reduced and there is little evidence of traffic. The engine shed (coded 31C), which had an allocation of 47 locomotives in 1950, was closed to steam in April 1959 when the remaining locomotives were transferred to South Lynn (the M&GNJR's shed in the town) and was demolished when it was closed completely two years later. Elsewhere, the passage of time has been less favourable to King's Lynn; the Hunstanton branch is closed completely, the Dereham branch curtailed to serve a sand quarry at Middleton Towers and the M&GNJR closed completely (except for a certain amount of freight from South Lynn accessed via the ex-GER line). (**A31881/670536**)

LANCASTER

Then: 9 May 1963
Now: 8 August 1997

Situated at the estuary of the River Lune, Lancaster was served by the lines of two of the pre-Grouping companies, the Midland and the London & North Western. All the lines passed to the LMSR in 1923 and to the London Midland Region of British Railways in 1948. This view, looking from south to north, shows in the foreground the LNWR yards to the south of the Castle station (1). From the station it is possible to see the overhead catenary of the MR electrification scheme on the link line to Green Ayre station (not illustrated, but to the east of the photograph). The electrified MR route across the Lune bridge (2) can be seen heading towards Morecambe and Heysham, whilst the LNWR West Coast main line heads north over the Lune (3). Adjacent to the junction with the MR line towards Green Ayre (4) is the junction for the line towards Glasson Dock (5). Hidden by the riverfront warehouses,

the quay at this point was also rail-served, access being achieved via the Glasson branch.

The railway was opened between Preston and Lancaster on 25 June 1840. The line north to Kendal was opened under the auspices of the Lancaster & Carlisle Railway on 22 September 1846. It was the L&CR that built the first Castle station, the line from Preston initially serving a terminus to the south. The first section of the line to Morecambe, from Green Ayre to Poulton, opened on 12 June 1848. The line from Wennington to Green Ayre opened on 17 November 1849 and was extended to Castle station on 19 December of the same year. The final extension was the branch to Glasson Dock, which opened for freight in April 1883 and to passenger services on 9 July of the same year. Electrification of the Green Ayre-Castle/Morecambe lines came in 1908 with services to

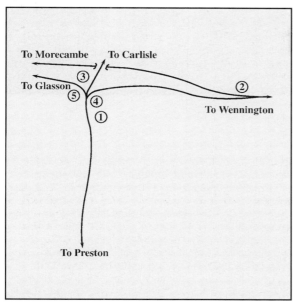

To Morecambe   To Carlisle

To Glasson ③

To Glasson ⑤   ④   ② To Wennington

①

To Preston

Morecambe commencing on 1 July and those to Castle on the following 14 September. The voltage was 6.6kV; by the date of the 'Then' photograph, the original 25 cycle equipment had been replaced, during the early 1950s, by 50 cycle equipment, although the voltage remained 6.6kV.

Today, Lancaster is served only by the electrified West Coast main line. Castle station remains but the associated trackwork has been much rationalised. The line to Glasson Docks lost its passenger services on 5 July 1930 but survived for freight until 5 October 1964; the junction at Castle remained in use until 30 June 1969 when the link to the quay was closed. On 3 January 1966 passenger services between Wennington and Morecambe and Green Ayre and Castle were withdrawn. The section of ex-MR line across the Lune between Green Ayre and White Lund closed completely on 5 June 1967. The final section of the ex-MR route to lose its services was the link between Castle and Green Ayre, which was closed completely on 17 March 1976. There are traces of the closed routes visible through the increased vegetation; off the 'Now' photograph on the right the old Lune bridge has been converted into a second road bridge across the Lune serving the town. (**A111498/670561**)

LEAMINGTON SPA

Then: 5 June 1958
Now: 9 September 1997

The Warwickshire town of Leamington Spa was served by both the Great Western and London & North Western railways. The two stations, as is clearly evident in the 'Then' photograph were adjacent. The ex-LNWR Avenue station, with its wooden platform extension, was to the east of the GWR station and served a loop of the LNWR running from Coventry to Rugby. The GWR station, pictured with a three car DMU in the up platform, was rebuilt between 1936 and 1939 at which time the impressive station facade was completed; the station served trains on the GWR main line from Birmingham (Snow Hill) to Paddington. The first railway to serve Leamington was the line from Coventry to Warwick (Milverton), which opened on 9 December 1844; this line was extended to Leamington on 27 July 1846 and thence to Rugby on 1 March 1851. The GWR line from Oxford to Birmingham opened on 1 October 1852. A junction between the two railways was established at the west end

of Leamington on 26 January 1864. The lines passed through LMS/GWR ownership before passing to BR; on 1 February 1958 the Western Region took charge of the Leamington Spa (Avenue)-Warwick (Milverton) section.

The process of rationalisation, as revealed in the reduced provision in the 'Now' photograph, started shortly after the 'Then' photograph was taken. On 15 September 1958 passenger services were withdrawn between Leamington Spa (Avenue) and Weedon; this was followed on 15 June 1959 by the cessation of passenger services from Avenue to Rugby; the ex-LNWR line survived as a freight route until complete closure between Leamington and Marton Junction on 4 April 1966.

Leamington Spa (Avenue) closed when passenger services to Coventry (and thence to Nuneaton) were withdrawn on 18 January 1965. Again, however, the line was retained for freight. A new junction between the ex-LNWR and ex-GWR lines at Leamington was opened on 15 May 1966 and it is over this line that the restored (from 2 May 1977) services from Coventry now operate. As can be seen, little remains of the LNWR side of this location; further south there are remains of the trackbed but these disappear once the former route heads eastwards towards Marton Junction. The ex-GWR station remains largely unchanged even if the car park at the front is busier. (**A71252/671397**)

LEEDS

Then: 17 September 1962
Now: 9 March 1998

Viewed looking towards the east, the complex arrangement of lines at the west of Leeds is clearly shown. In the foreground (1) the ex-Midland line through the Aire Valley and the ex-North Eastern line from Harrogate approach from the northwest. At Geldard Junction (2) the Great Northern & North Eastern Joint section approaches the three goods yards at Wellington Street; these yards were owned by the NER (3), the GNR (4) and jointly by the London & North Western and Lancashire & Yorkshire (5).

Alongside is Central station (6), which was jointly controlled by the GNR, the NER, the LYR and the LNWR. The passenger line came through Three Signal Bridge Junction (7), with its link to Geldard Junction, before passing through Holbeck High Level station (8). Beneath High Level station was Holbeck Low Level (9), through which the ex-MR line passed *en route* to Holbeck Junction (10) and Whitehall Junction (11). At the latter, a connection to the LNWR at Copley Hill Junction came in; this route

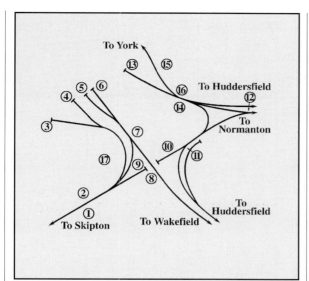

provided access to the LYR/LNWR goods yard at Whitehall Road. The ex-MR Leeds avoiding line heads from Whitehall Junction to Engine Shed Junction (12), whilst the ex-MR line towards Wellington station (13) heads through Leeds Junction (14), where the ex-MR line from Engine Shed Junction approaches from the southwest. Alongside Wellington station is New station (15),which was jointly controlled by the LNWR and the NER; the former approached Leeds via the viaduct route from North Junction at Farnley. Wellington and New stations were combined on 2 may 1938 under the single name of 'Leeds City'. At Canal Junction (16), there was also a connection between the LNWR/NER joint line and the MR approaches to Wellington. Also visible (17) is the ex-NER locomotive roundhouse.

There has been, as is all too evident in the 'Now'photograph, considerable rationalisation in Leeds over the past 30 years. The major change came with the decision in 1963 to concentrate all of city's passenger services into a rebuilt City station — replacing the old 'New' station — which was completed in mid-1967. (**A105866/673514**)

LEICESTER

Then: undated (c1952)
Now: 16 August 1997

This view, taken looking north from Leicester Midland station shows in detail the Leicester Midland shed, which was rebuilt in 1952. The 32-road roundhouse was home to 80 steam locomotives in 1950 and to 63 in 1959. Coded 15B from Nationalisation until 1963 and 15A thereafter. There are in excess of 10 locomotives visible around the original coaling stage. This was replaced as part of the rebuilding process and this fact, combined with the fact that the locomotives are lettered either 'LMS' or 'British Railways', implies a date for the photograph of around 1952. Also visible to the west of the main line northwards are, closest to the main line, the ex-Midland Railway goods yard and, beyond it, the ex-LNWR yard. The main line, which was later to form part of the Midland main line, was first opened between Leicester and Trent Junction on 5 May 1840 courtesy of the Midland Counties Railway.

The Midland main line continues to provide an important route today, although much of the infrastructure illustrated in the 'Then' photograph has disappeared.

Leicester Midland lost its steam allocation in 1966, although it remained operational as a diesel depot. The roundhouse was partially demolished after closure and today the site is used partly as a locomotive stabling point — and four locomotives can be seen stabled in front of the depot (now coded 'LR') — and partly as the location of Leicester's new power signalbox; this was constructed from 1984 and on 29 June 1986 replaced 12 manual boxes in the so-called 'Leicester Gap'. Also now but a memory is the enormous goods warehouse on the west of the line; as so often is the case, this facility has been replaced by a new shopping precinct. (A24247/670443)

LINCOLN

Then: 20 August 1964
Now: 4 September 1997

The cathedral city of Lincoln was served by the trains of three pre-Grouping companies — the Midland, the Great Northern and the Great Central — as well as the GN&GE Joint, which provided access for Great Eastern services from East Anglia. This excellent view shows the complex network of lines in the period before major rationalisation. The two passenger stations — Central (ex-GN; 1) and St Marks (ex-GC/MR; 2) — are clearly visible as are the lines towards Nottingham (ex-MR; 3), Gainsborough (ex-GN&GE Jt; 4), to Grimsby (ex-GC; 5) and to Boston and Sleaford (ex-GN/ex-GN&GE Jt; 6). Freight facilities included the ex-GC West goods yard (7), the ex-GN goods yard (8), the ex-MR goods yard (9), the ex-GC East goods yard (10), Durham Ox Junction (11) and Pelham Street level crossing (12). Further to the west, and not shown, was the ex-GN&GE Jt avoiding line. The first line to serve Lincoln was the future Midland Railway line from

Newark, which opened on 3 August 1846. This was followed on 17 October 1848 by the Great Northern's line from Boston. The line towards Market Rasen opened on 18 December 1848 and that to Gainsborough on 9 April 1849. Eighteen years was to elapse before the opening of the line from Sincil Junction towards Grantham on 15 April 1867. This was followed on 1 December 1876 by the opening of the line to Louth via Bardney. The last major line to reach Lincoln was the Lancashire, Derbyshire & East Coast (late GCR) line from Chesterfield, which opened on 8 March 1897.

At the time of the 'Then' photograph there had been some minor losses; passenger services over the Louth line were withdrawn on 5 November 1951, those over the LDECR route on 19 September 1955, those from Retford on 2 November 1959 and those from Boston on 17 October 1963. However, as elsewhere, major changes

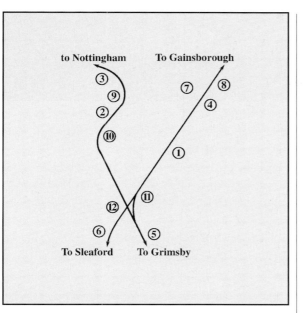

were to take place in the 1960s and after. The Grantham line lost its passenger services on 1 November 1965 and the Firsby line saw services withdrawn on 5 October 1970. However, despite these closures, Lincoln was still provided with two stations and the city was plagued with numerous level crossings. In the early 1980s, it was decided to concentrate services on Central station and close St Marks. A new connection was installed from the Newark line on to the avoiding line. This enabled passenger services to be withdrawn from St Marks on 12 May 1985, at which time the line through St Marks to the East goods yard closed completely. The final section, from Durham Ox Junction to the coal depot at East closed on 15 January 1989. Today, Lincoln is linked to Market Rasen, Sleaford, Newark and Gainsborough, with all passenger services through Central. As can be seen, traces of the former alignment through St Marks survive, as does the GNR-built Pelham Street Level Crossing signalbox. Lincoln Central station is largely unchanged, with the main building dating from the 1840s. In the centre foreground, between the Sleaford and Market Rasen lines, can be seen the tracks leading to the now-disused diesel depot. (**A138329/671611**)

LIVERPOOL

Then: 25 June 1955
Now: 9 August 1997

The famous Pier Head at Liverpool is captured at a time when both Liverpool Corporation's electric tramcars and the Liverpool Overhead Railway — the 'Dockers Umbrella' — were still operational. The Liverpool Overhead Railway ran, as its name implies, on an elevated platform from Dingle in the south to Seaforth in the north. The station in the right foreground at which a train is stopped is James Street; Pier Head station is hidden by the Liver Building, the northernmost of the three impressive buildings facing the Pier Head. The middle structure is the Cunard Building and the southernmost is the Dock Board. The Liverpool Overhead Railway was officially opened on 4 February 1893 by the Marquis of Salisbury. The Pier Head itself shows the complex of three loops that served Liverpool's once extensive tramway network; although much modernised in the 1930s — and the view shows a number of the Marks-designed streamlined trams delivered in that decade — a policy of tramcar abandonment was

adopted in the late 1940s and by the date of this photograph much of the tramway network had already been converted to bus operation. Also visible on the right, in the background, is Liverpool Exchange station, the Lancashire & Yorkshire Railway's station in the city, which was constructed in 1888 to replace an earlier structure.

Although, today, many of the most familiar landmarks in Liverpool — such as those at the Pier Head — remain, indeed many have been cleaned, and the Mersey ferries continue to ply their trade across to the Wirral, both the trams and the Overhead Railway have long since departed. The LOR was to close on 30 December 1956 and, despite efforts to get it reopened, the route was dismantled for scrap after September 1957. The last Liverpool trams operated on 14 September 1957. Even Liverpool Exchange is no more; the last services operating to the terminus on 30 April 1977. In the foreground, the Albert Docks complex is now home to museums rather than commercial traffic and the other docks illustrated here are also bereft of shipping. **(A59820/670571)**

LIVERPOOL STREET

Then: 1 November 1957
Now: 28 July 1997

If a week is a long time in politics, 40 years is an inordinate length of time in the City of London. This view shows the inter-relationship between the ex-Great Eastern Railway terminus of Liverpool Street with the ex-North London Railway station at Broad Street. The first part of Liverpool Street, covering the suburban services, was opened on 2 February 1874 and the remainder followed on 1 November 1875, at which date the earlier terminus at

Bishopgate was closed (although it remained open as a freight yard until the early 1960s). The station design was the work of the GER's engineer Edward Wilson. His station saw trackwork modification in 1890 and an eastward extension four years later. Broad Street was both slightly earlier and built at a higher level than Liverpool Street; it opened to passenger services on 1 November 1865 and to freight on 18 May 1868; the goods yard was

to the north (ie to the left here) of the passenger station. The North London Railway was taken over by the London & North Western in 1922. Broad Street was originally provided with seven platforms, but this was later increased to eight. The North London line was an early conversion to electric traction, being converted on 1 October 1916, with services running to Richmond.

The first proposals for the redevelopment of the area came in the late 1970s, but it was not until 1982 that approval was given to the British Rail Property Board's plans for the massive Broadgate redevelopment. Although initial plans were for the complete destruction of the 19th century Liverpool Street station, a campaign (led by the then Poet Laureate Sir John Betjeman) saw the original 1870s train shed both retained and sympathetically restored. Broad Street station was, however, less fortunate. Freight facilities at Broad Street had already been withdrawn (on 27 January 1969) and the passenger traffic

had been reduced with the transfer of the Richmond trains to serve North Woolwich leaving only peak hour services to Watford in May 1985. Formal closure of Broad Street was approved in June 1985 and demolition began in November that year, although the last passenger services did not operate until 30 June 1986 when the opening of the Graham Road curve allowed for the remaining services to be diverted into Liverpool Street. The 'Now' photograph shows the extent of the redevelopment well; there is now no trace of Broad Street station, although the disused trackbed can be seen stretching off towards Dalston in the background. The extended 1870s train shed at Liverpool Street with reproduction red-brick entry is evident as is the office development built over the 1890s extension to the station. For passengers using Liverpool Street, the retention of the train shed has ensured an airy and clean atmosphere, making Liverpool Street one of the more successful redevelopments of the past decade. **(A96827/669452)**

LOUGHBOROUGH

Then: 21 June 1938
Now: 4 September 1997

In the foreground the Great Central's London extension runs north towards Nottingham and south towards Loughborough and Leicester; this line opened to freight in 1898 and to passenger services on 9 March 1899. The Trent Junction-Loughborough-Leicester section of the Midland Counties (later Midland Railway) opened on 5 May 1840. The Brush Works, famous as manufacturers of railway locomotives and tramcars, was established on the site here in 1880.

The Great Central main line lost its through services on 5 September 1966. At the same time the sections between Aylesbury and Rugby Central and Nottingham Victoria and Sheffield saw all passenger services withdrawn. The section between Rugby and Nottingham via

Loughborough was to soldier on for a further three years until these services were also withdrawn (on 5 May 1969). Efforts by the Main Line Steam Trust saw the section south of Loughborough as far as the northern outskirts of Leicester eventually preserved, but the bridge at Loughborough was demolished. The section from Loughborough north to Ruddington (on the southern outskirts of Nottingham) was retained for freight, access being gained by a new spur shown clearly in the 'Now' photograph. The Ruddington-Hotchley Hill section was closed in the early 1980s and the line north from Loughborough to Hotchley Hill is now disused. The modern Great Central, based at Loughborough, has taken over the site at Ruddington and intends to restore services over the line southwards to Loughborough Central; this will include, eventually, the construction of a replacement bridge over the ex-Midland main line. The Brush Works, albeit with some changes (notice the demise of the ornate entrance, for example) is still busy. Recent work has included the construction of the Class 60 diesel-electrics. **(C12634/671620)**

LOWESTOFT

Then: 31 May 1963
Now: 11 August 1997

Primarily a major port, Lowestoft was served by both the Great Eastern and Midland & Great Northern railways, the latter reaching the town courtesy of the Norfolk & Suffolk Joint Line from Great Yarmouth. Visible here are Coke Ovens Junction (1), the point at which the N&S Joint line came in from the north, Central station (2) and evidence of the rail-served harbour on the south side of Lake Lothing (3). The line ran on beyond Central station to serve the fish market (4). Lowestoft shed (32C) was located further inland to the west. The first railway to reach Lowestoft

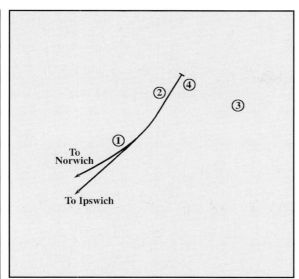

linked the town with Reedham on the Norwich-Yarmouth line; this branch opened to freight on 3 May 1847 and to passengers on the following 1 July. A second line, reaching Lowestoft from the south via Carlton Colville, was opened on 1 June 1859; at the same time the freight-only branch serving Kirkley and the harbour was also opened. The Norfolk & Suffolk Joint line opened on 13 July 1903.

Passenger services over the line to Great Yarmouth were withdrawn on 4 May 1970 (at which time the line was closed completely); today there is no evidence of the junction or of the joint line heading north. The line serving the south side of Lake Lothing (to Kirkley) was closed completely on 6 November 1967. Although there is evidence of much commercial activity on the south side, none of it is rail-served. Lowestoft retains DMU services to Norwich and to Ipswich over the East Suffolk line. The station survives as well, but it has been much rationalised over the years. Civil Engineers' sidings and a small amount of freight survive in addition, but Lowestoft's status has declined greatly since 1963. **(A113137/670529)**

LUTON

Then: 9 September 1964
Now: 10 September 1997

The Bedfordshire town of Luton was served by the lines of two companies — the Midland and the Great Northern. The stations serving the two routes were, as is clearly visible here, adjacent. On the extreme left is the ex-Midland Railway station whilst at a slightly lower level can be seen Luton (Bute Street), which served the ex-GNR line from Dunstable to Welwyn. In the distance the Midland main line can be seen heading southwards towards London and a four-car DMU can be seen. At this time there was no physical connection between the ex-MR and ex-GNR lines; this was only constructed when the ex-GNR line east of Luton was closed completely, opening on 3 January 1966. The first stretch of line serving Luton to open was the link westwards to Dunstable, which opened on 3 May 1858; this line met the London & North Western branch from Leighton Buzzard at Dunstable and

for the first two years of the line's life it was operated by the LNWR. GNR operation only commenced with the opening of the line eastwards towards Welwyn on 1 September 1860. The Midland Railway through the town was opened with the MR's London extension from Bedford to St Pancras (to freight on 8 September 1867, passenger services to Moorgate on 13 July 1868 and services to St Pancras on 1 October 1868). The ex-MR station illustrated here was rebuilt between 1937 and 1940. Apart from the two stations, also visible are the considerable freight facilities provided for the town; Luton was a major centre of hat manufacturing (reflected in the fact that the local football team is nicknamed 'The Hatters').

Passenger services over the line between Leighton Buzzard and Hatfield were withdrawn in two stages: from Leighton Buzzard to Dunstable on 2 July 1962 and thence, via Bute Street, to Hatfield on 26 April 1965 (shortly after the 'Then' photograph was taken). The section of the ex-GNR line from Luton South towards

Welwyn closed completely on 3 January 1966 at which time the new spur was opened. This allowed continued access to Dunstable for freight; apart from the Vauxhall works at Dunstable there was also a rail-served concrete works. The 1966 spur and the Dunstable branch were mothballed from 30 April 1989. Today the site of Bute Street station is part of the car park serving the surviving ex-Midland station; the trackbed for the Dunstable line has been severed, although the rusting lines still run over the bridge in the foreground. There have been a number of proposals for the reopening of the line — including the possibility of a rapid transit scheme — but these have all failed to materialise. The long-term future of the route looks insecure. The ex-Midland line, however, continues to prosper. Suburban services to Bedford were electrified in 1983; apart from these services the line sees main line services linking St Pancras with the midlands and north. A new station is to be built slightly to the south to serve the increasingly important airport at Luton.
(A138639/672801)

MALLAIG

Then: 31 August 1964
Now: 14 April 1998

Whilst most railways in Britain were built by private undertakings with little or no official encouragement, the West Highland line from Fort William to Mallaig, built to assist the fishing industry, was supported financially by the government of the day, which also contributed £30,000 to the construction of a breakwater and pier at Mallaig.

The line opened on 1 April 1901. The 'Then' shot shows clearly the relationship between the station, single-road locomotive shed, pier and breakwater. No less than four Type 2 (later Class 27) diesel-electric locomotives are visible; these locomotives, based at Eastfield, were synonymous with the West Highland line until their final

withdrawal in 1987. In steam days, Mallaig shed was a subshed of Fort William. The signalbox visible dates from the opening of the line and is one of 17 ex-NBR boxes that survived on the national network at the end of 1996 from the 641 that passed to the LNER in 1923.

From the opening of the line, the North British Railway appreciated that the Mallaig line offered considerable potential as a tourist line. Although the sleeper service from King's Cross was shortlived — being later terminated at Fort William — through coaches were run from King's Cross. The LNER operated rail cruises from 1933, which included a run over the Mallaig line, whilst Observation Cars also operated over the route under both the LNER and BR. Today, the line is host to steam specials regularly running between Fort William and Mallaig, as well as normal passenger services. As can be seen, the facilities at Mallaig have been rationalised, with the disappearance of the platform awnings, the engine shed, turntable and signalbox. Along the foreshor, a new road has been built and this, together with the railway, can be seen stretching into the distance through the beautiful Highlands countryside. (**A138851/651525**)

MANCHESTER

Then: 12 June 1969
Now: 4 May 1998

Viewed looking northeastwards, in the foreground can be seen the ex-London & North Western Exchange station (1). This is linked to the ex-Lancashire & Yorkshire Victoria station (2) by a covered through platform. The impressive facade of the ex-L&YR station is clearly visible as are through platforms on the northern side of the station. Immediately to the northeast of Victoria station, the line towards Bury heads north (3) past the

Red Bank carriage sidings (4) and the Queens Road carriage sidings (5) to Cheetham Hill Junction (6), where the line splits, with one route heading on towards Bury and the second towards Rochdale. Also visible at this point are the Cheetham Hill carriage sidings (7). The main line continues to run northeastwards past the Newtown carriage sidings (8) and the short tunnel for the alternative route to Bury under the main line (9).

This route to Bury can be seen heading towards Queens Road Junction (10), where it connects into a curve from Cheetham Hill Junction. To the east can be seen the Oldham Road goods depot (11) and the route out towards Oldham Road Junction (12). Finally, it is just possible to locate the important junction at Miles Platting in the distance (13).

The contemporary scene shows how radical the changes can be in even a major city like Manchester. Although the basic railway network can still be identified — the line runs through Victoria from the southwest towards Miles Platting, the route from Manchester Victoria East Junction continues to operate past the siding at Red Bank (albeit only as a freight or diversionary line) — much is different. Manchester Exchange closed on 5

May 1969 (ironically one month before the 'Then' photograph and was subsequently demolished. The through platforms at Victoria were rationalised and largely demolished during the early 1990s with a new sports arena built over the remaining through platforms. The main station facade has been restored, but the number of terminal platforms have been reduced. Partly this is the result of the conversion of the Bury line to form part of the new Manchester Metrolink tramway system; this opened in 1992 and, for the first time, provides a direct link between Victoria and Piccadilly stations. The former carriage sidings at Queens Road have been converted into the Metrolink depot and workshops. The goods yard at Oldham Road closed during the 1980s. (**SV2058/673909**)

MERTHYR TYDFIL

Then: 16 September 1955
Now: 13 September 1997

During the mid and late 19th century a complex network of lines was built by various competing railway companies to serve the industrial Welsh Valleys. One of the most important settlements in the valleys was Merthyr Tydfil, which was served by a number of lines, including the Taff Vale and the Vale of Neath railways, both of which eventually passed into GWR ownership. The TVR opened its branch from Abercynon in 1841, although this route followed the alignment of the earlier horse-powered

Merthyr Tramroad. The Vale of Neath arrived in 1853 and until 1877 the railway maintained separate stations. In that year services were concentrated on the Vale of Neath station (as illustrated in the centre of this photograph), the TVR station becoming the site of the Plymouth Street goods station (illustrated at the top right of this photograph). Also visible towards the centre top of the photograph is the three-road engine shed that served Merthyr. The shed, coded 88D between 1948 and closure

in 1964, was built by the GWR on the site of the earlier Vale of Neath Railway shed. In 1955 the shed had an allocation of 55 locomotives. Of these the bulk were '56xx' 0-6-2Ts or 0-6-0PTs of either '57xx' or '64xx' classes, but there were also 15 0-6-2Ts of Taff Vale or Rhymney Railway origin. The five-platform station possessed an overall roof designed by Brunel, but this had already been replaced by the date of the 'Then' photograph, being dismantled in 1953. Adjacent to the station are the granary and goods warehouses.

Although passenger services continue to serve Merthyr Tydfil over the ex-Taff Vale (now single track) branch from Pontypridd, the majority of passenger services that once used Merthyr Tydfil High Street disappeared during the 1950s and 1960s. As a result, the station at Merthyr Tydfil was initially rationalised — the westernmost platform (No 1) being closed in 1959 — before being completely rebuilt in 1971 at which time the signalbox was abolished, the line becoming single track at that stage. Today, the station has been rebuilt once more, replacing the somewhat utilitarian structure of 1971 with a single platform and new buildings. The site of the goods yard has become a carpark, whilst the locomotive shed has also been redeveloped. The Plymouth Street goods yard finally closed on 27 November 1967 and there is now nothing to indicate its presence. (R25342/671363)

MONMOUTH
(MAY HILL)

Then: 27 August 1932
Now: 19 November 1997

This was one of two stations constructed by the Great Western Railway to serve the small town. Monmouth is situated alongside the River Wye. Monmouth was first served by a tramroad linking the town with Cinderford, but it was not until 2 October 1857 that the Coleford Monmouth Usk & Pontypool Road Railway opened to Monmouth Troy. Monmouth May Hill station opened on 4 August 1873 when the line to Ross on Wye was opened; it was completed through to Monmouth Troy on the following 1 August. The Wye Valley line from Monmouth to Chepstow opened on 11 August 1876.

Although there is much that can be directly compared, there is little that now survives to indicate that there was

once a railway at this location — even the road overbridge has been removed. The first casualty was the complete closure of the line from Monmouth Troy to Pontypool Road, which occurred on 13 June 1955 (officially; services actually ceased earlier due to an ASLEF dispute). The line from Troy to Ross on Wye via May Hill closed completely on 5 January 1959, with the exception of the short section from Troy to May Hill which remained until freight facilities were withdrawn in October 1963. Also withdrawn on 5 January 1959 were passenger services over the line from Troy to Chepstow; freight, however, continued to operate to Troy until the complete closure of the line north from Tintern on 6 January 1964. **(39977/672897)**

NEWCASTLE

Then: Undated
Now: 23 October 1997

This striking view shows the River Tyne running from west to east with, on its north bank, Newcastle Central station (1). Newcastle's castle, with its famous and complex junction, can be seen to the east of the station (2) with the East Coast main line heading towards Morpeth (3). Amongst the bridges spanning the Tyne are the two railway bridges — King Edward (4) and High Level (5) — whilst the line towards Sunderland can be seen heading southeastwards (6). Gateshead station is located, but cannot easily be seen, at the southern side of the High Level bridge, whilst Gateshead shed (coded 52A by British Railways; 7) stands alongside the line south of the Tyne with the former NER workshops between it and the river. The foreground of the scene is dominated by the enormous Forth Street goods yard (8). This was originally opened in 1871 and extended in 1892/93. The easternmost end of the warehouse was cut back when the King

Edward bridge was constructed. Running from Central station, on the north side of Forth Street, is the old Newcastle & Carlisle main line towards Scotswood (9).

Although predated by the Newcastle & North Shields (which opened on 22 June 1839 from Manors to North Shields and was extended to Central station on 1 September 1848), it was the opening of the Newcastle & Carlisle that set the city towards becoming a major railway intersection. This line opened from Scotswood into Newcastle on 21 October 1839; the line was extended to Forth on 1 March 1847 and thence to Central station on 1 January 1851. The first railway bridge across the Tyne was the High Level, upon which work started in 1846 and the first line across opened on 15 August 1849. On 28 September 1849 the royal train conveying Queen Victoria ran across the bridge and this is generally regarded as marking the formal opening of the bridge.

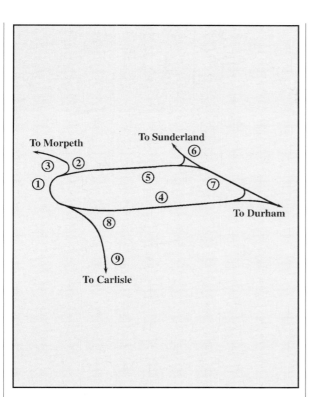

High Level bridge was designed by Robert Stephenson and T. E. Harrison. The construction of the bridge enabled through trains to operate, but until the opening of the King Edward bridge on 10 July 1906, through trains had to reverse at Newcastle. Gateshead Works was originally the main locomotive works of the NER, but locomotive construction ceased in 1910; locomotives continued to be overhauled at Gateshead until 1932 and resumed when required during World War 2. Complete closure came in 1959 and the site was cleared in the late 1960s.

Today, Newcastle Central station remains, although there has been rationalisation. The trainshed roof and the main building (of 1850 and 1860) survive, although again there have been internal changes. A third railway bridge has been added to the Tyne, with the official opening on 6 November 1981 of the Queen Elizabeth bridge to serve the new Metro. The enormous Forth Street goods yard has closed; the buildings were demolished some time before the final closure in 1983; only some civil engineers' sidings remain to remind people of the once impressive railway presence here. The old Newcastle & Carlisle line from Central to Blaydon saw its passenger service transferred to the line along the south of the Tyne (see Blaydon) and was closed completely between Blaydon and Elswich on 4 October 1982. A rusting line past the site of Forth Street goods is all that remains of this once important cross-country line. (C19121/672582)

NEWPORT
(GWENT)

Then: 14 September 1929
Now: 16 August 1997

Viewed looking east across the River Usk, a freight train (1) makes its stately progress on the line towards Chepstow and Gloucester. In the foreground a passenger train (2) awaits departure from Newport station with a westbound service towards Cardiff; note that the consist includes a number of clerestory coaches. Dominating the centre of the photograph is Newport High Street station (3), whilst in the distance can be seen Maindee West Junction and the line northwards to Pontypool. Evidence

of the alternative line towards Pontypool up the west side of the Usk can be seen (4; 5). In the foreground are Godfrey Road sidings (6). The main line from Chepstow to Swansea was opened on 18 June 1850. The first link to Pontypool was that up the west bank of the Usk, which opened in 1853. The route via Maindee West Junction was opened in 1874. The station illustrated in the 'Then' photograph was rebuilt during the 1930s.

Newport remains an important station on the main line

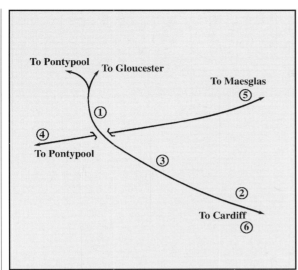

from Cardiff eastwards. The station remains largely unchanged from the rebuilding of the 1930s, although the adjacent goods shed has disappeared. Also now closed is the line running on the west side of the Usk towards Pontypool, although this is still open at the southern end to serve the coal depot at Dock Street. The line closed completely between Cymbran and Newport Mill Street on 27 October 1963 and between Mill Street and Dock Street on 28 November 1966. Godfrey Road Sidings, however, survive as a locomotive stabling point. (29304/670337)

NEWPORT
(ISLE OF WIGHT)

Then: 1 September 1928
Now: 17 November 1997

With routes radiating out to the north (towards Cowes; opened 16 June 1862), to the east (towards Smallbrook Junction; opened 20 December 1875), to the south (towards Sandown and Ventnor; opened 6 October 1875 to a temporary terminus, being linked to the Ryde & Newport via an expensive viaduct on 1 June 1879) and to the west (towards Freshwater; opened to freight on 10 September 1888 and to passengers on 20 July 1889), Newport was one of the most important junctions on the small and isolated Isle of Wight railway network. With the exception of the line to Freshwater, which was operated by the Freshwater, Yarmouth & Newport Railway (following the collapse of an agreement with the IoWCR), all the other lines serving Newport were originally operated by the Isle of Wight Central Railway (although having all their origins in earlier companies and being unified on 1 July 1887). The Isle of Wight operators were incorporated into the Southern Railway during 1923.

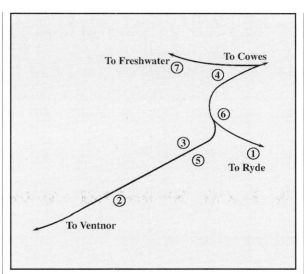

At the date of the 'Then' photograph, it is possible to see (1) the line heading in from the east (Smallbrook Junction), (2) the line from Ventnor crossing over the viaduct (3) that had proved costly to construct. The central station (4) is visible in the background along with the line westwards to Freshwater (7).

Taking the terrace of houses (5) as a reference point, it becomes clear that today very little remains to indicate that Newport was once a railway junction. Passenger services over the line to Ventnor West ceased on 15 September 1952, those to Freshwater on 21 September 1953 (the line closing completely) and those to Sandown on 6 February 1956 (closing the line south from Newport completely), leaving those linking Cowes with Smallbrook Junction to survive until 21 February 1966 (when the line closed completely). In the 30 years since this last closure occurred, the route that the railway once took has become utilised for a major road; it is interesting to note that the new road perpetuates the junction between the Sandown and Ryde lines (6). **(23022/672835)**

NEWTON STEWART

Then: August 1930
Now: 4 November 1997

Situated on the Portpatrick & Wigtownshire Joint line from Castle Douglas to Port Stewart, Newton Stewart was the junction for the branches southwards to Whithorn and Garlieston. The P&WJR was controlled by four of the pre-Grouping companies — the Caledonian, the Glasgow &

South Western, the Midland and the London & North Western — which meant that it passed to sole LMS control in 1923. The line was opened throughout from Castle Douglas to Stranraer on 12 March 1861. The branch from Newton Stewart to Wigtown followed on

160

3 April 1875. The branch was extended from Wigtown to Millisle on 2 August 1875 and thence to Garlieston on 3 April 1876 and from Millisle to Whithorn on 9 July 1877. The section from Millisle to Garlieston lost its passenger services as long ago as 1 March 1903. The 'Then' shot shows clearly the station, the junction for the line south towards Wigtown, the signalboxes as well as the goods yard. Whithorn services departed from the north side of the island platform.

Today, although the railway has long gone, it is still possible to see considerable evidence from the air to illustrate where it once ran. Passenger services over the Whithorn branch were withdrawn on 25 September 1950, although freight over this line and the short branch to Garlieston continued for a further decade, until the branch south from Newton Stewart was closed completely on 5 October 1964. This was, however, just a precursor to the closure of the 'Port Road' from Dumfries to Stranraer on 14 June 1965. It is possible to make out in the 'Now' photograph the trackbed and station site, although the latter is partially occupied with industrial units. Also evident is the extent to which the town has grown over the past 65 years; no doubt much of this growth has occurred in the decades since the line closed. (**34401/672639**)

NORTHAMPTON

Then: 28 March 1968
Now: 24 October 1997

This view, looking north, shows the complex arrangement of lines approaching Northampton from the south. Although all the lines illustrated here were formerly owned by the London & North Western, Northampton was also served by the Midland Railway from the south; the ex-MR facilities were to the east of the area illustrated here (although the ex-MR St John's Street station lost its passenger services in July 1939 when they were transferred to the ex-LNWR station). Illustrated in this view are the ex-LNWR line stretching towards Rugby (1), Castle station (2), Roade Line Junction (3) at which a 25kV locomotive is visible, the ex-LNWR route towards London (4), Duston North Junction (5) with lines heading towards Duston West Junction and Blisworth (6) and towards Bridge Street Junction and Peterborough (7). Notice also the rail-served gas works (8) and oil depot (9).

Despite its importance, Northampton was bypassed by the original London & Birmingham Railway, and it was not until 31 May 1845 that the L&BR opened its branch from Blisworth; this was extended to Peterborough on 2 June 1845. The line from Bridge Street Junction — where the town's original station was sited — through the future Castle station, where a small station was built at this time, to Market Harborough was opened on 16 February 1859. The MR reached Northampton in 1866 using running powers over the LNWR; its own route was not opened until 1872. The Roade-Northampton-Rugby section was a development of the 1880s and was linked to the quadrupling of the line south from Roade towards London; the lines through Northampton being treated as the 'slow' route. The section between Northampton and Rugby opened on 1 December 1881 and that between Northampton and Roade on 3 April 1882. Additional work at the time included the purchase (and demolition) of the old castle and the construction of a new goods shed (10) upon the site and the rebuilding of Castle station.

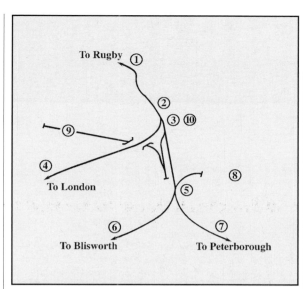

Another major development, in 1933, was the building of a major marshalling yard (10) north of the station. The Rugby-Northampton-Roade line was electrified in the mid-1960s, with a new timetable being inaugurated on 18 April 1966.

By the date of the 'Then' photograph, Northampton's railways had already been rationalised; passenger services over the lines to Market Harborough and Blisworth had been withdrawn on 4 January 1960, whilst those over the route to Peterborough followed on 6 May 1964. The line from Duston North Junction to Blisworth closed completely on 6 January 1969 and that to Market Harborough on 31 May 1980. Today, Northampton is served by passenger services over the electrified route; Castle station remains, although the adjacent goods yard has been much reduced with the building replaced by a carpark. North of the station, the 1933 marshalling yard is discernible, although clearly out of use. A single track — the rump of the line towards Peterborough — stretches down from Roade Line Junction to serve facilities in the Bridge Street area. (**A179958/672927**)

NORWICH

Then: 10 June 1966
Now: 11 August 1997

Pictured here are the approaches to the main station in Norwich in the period immediately after steam operation. Pictured are Thorpe station (1), the tracks leading to the goods station (2), the engine shed (3), old locomotive works (4), the loop line (5), the main line heading towards Trowse (6), Thorpe Junction (7), Wensum Junction (8) and the line towards Great Yarmouth (9). The first railway to serve Norwich was the Yarmouth & Norwich, which opened on 30 April 1844. The line from Trowse was opened 15 December 1845 with the completion of the swing bridge. Both lines were eventually to form part of the Great Eastern Railway. The future main line to Ipswich and London opened on 12 December 1849 (and served Victoria station); it was not until 1852 that a link was established that allowed services from Ipswich to reach Thorpe station; Victoria station lost its passenger

164

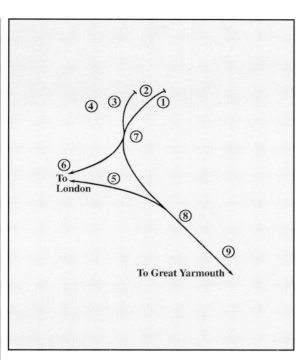

services on 22 May 1916 but remained as a freight depot until final closure. Norwich was also served by a branch of the M&GNJR, which ran into City station. The present-day Norwich Thorpe station was built in 1886 to the design of John Wilson and W. N. Ashbee.

The locomotive shed at Norwich dates back to the era of the Yarmouth & Norwich Railway, and the old locomotive works housed an erecting shop. Until the early 1930s, Norwich was capable of handling most heavy maintenance work. Under BR the shed was classified 32A; it was a large facility that housed 130 locomotives in 1950 and 93 in 1959. In its later years it was to play host to many of the Eastern Region's 'Britannia' class Pacifics. The shed lost its steam allocation in 1962, but survived modernisation to house the replacement diesels.

Today, Norwich Thorpe remains active (although the adjacent goods shed has been demolished). The locomotive shed survived until electrification and the opening of the new Crown Point maintenance depot seen in the foreground. The shed, despite its antiquity, has been demolished. Also now disappeared is the huge engineering workshop that was located to the north of Norwich City's Carrow Road ground. Services over the line from Ipswich are now electric (from 11 May 1987), but diesel power is still the order of the day over the lines towards Cromer, Ely and Great Yarmouth. (A184919/670503)

NOTTINGHAM

Then: 19 June 1961
Now: 16 August 1997

The city of Nottingham, traditional home of the British lace industry, was served by three of the great pre-Grouping railway companies — the Midland, the Great Northern and the Great Central. This view, taken looking southeastwards, shows to good effect the relationship between the lines of these three companies. The GN/GC station, Victoria, is off to the north through the 393yd-long Victoria Street tunnel; Weekday Cross Junction (1) sees the GNR route heading towards London Road (High Level) station (2) whilst the GCR route heads southwards over the MR station (3) before approaching Arkwright Street station (slightly to the south of the area illustrated). Also visible are London Road (Low Level) goods yard (4) and the MR's goods yards and grain warehouse (built 1896) (5).

The first railway to serve Nottingham was the Midland Counties Railway — later to form part of the Midland — which opened its link between the two cities on 29 May 1839. From this the MR developed a network of lines

serving the city and its environs. The Great Northern reached Nottingham from Grantham (courtesy of the Ambergate, Nottingham & Boston & Eastern Junction Railway) on 15 July 1850; services initially operated into the Midland's station, but the GNR opened its own station (London Road) on 3 October 1857. The Great Central's London Extension was constructed during the 1890s; the first coal trains operated southwards over the route on 26 July 1898 and the first passenger services on the following 15 March. Nottingham Victoria station was officially opened on 24 May 1900. The link between the GN and GC routes was also constructed; this allowed GNR services to be transferred from London Road (Low Level) via a new London Road (High Level) station into the new station; Low Level was officially closed for passenger services on 22 May 1944. The Midland Railway's response to the opening of the GC was to rebuild its own station; work started in mid-1903 and the

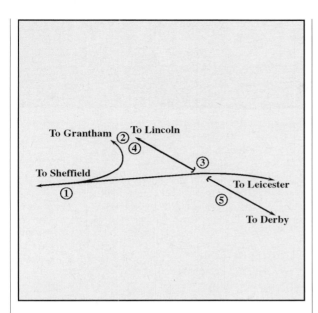

GNR routes, although there are odd traces visible upon careful inspection; London Road (High Level) station has disappeared although London Road (Low Level) still stands, albeit devoid of track, after a period as a parcels depot. The work to demolish the viaducts took in a piecemeal fashion after the lines closed; in 1978, for example, the bridge across London Road was removed and in May 1980 work to remove the viaduct over the Midland station commenced. Through services over the ex-GC main line ceased on 5 September 1966, when services north of Victoria station to Sheffield were withdrawn. Nottingham Victoria was the terminus of the line from Rugby until these were curtailed at Arkwright Street on 4 September 1967; at the same time passenger services ceased to serve the ex-GNR route to Victoria. Although the site at Victoria was being demolished, freight continued through the station to serve Colwick yard until 26 May 1968. Passenger services over the Rugby-Arkwright Street section were withdrawn on 5 May 1969, but the lines through London Road (High Level), Weekday Cross Junction and Arkwright Street remained to provide access to the Ruddington MoD depot until a new connection between the ex-MR and ex-GCR lines was constructed in 1974; this link allowed for the depot to be served from the south and for the closure of the remaining section of the ex-GNR/GCR routes in central Nottingham from 8 April 1974. Elsewhere the Midland station still survives, although the large goods and grain warehouse has disappeared (demolished in 1992 to be replaced by new offices for the Inland Revenue). **(A90961/670373)**

new station, designed by A. E. Lambert, was provided with a dramatic facade on to Carrington Street.

The changes in Nottingham over the past 30 years are probably as dramatic as those that occurred in the 1890s; indeed the period has seen almost the complete reversal of the construction of that time. Almost completely demolished are the viaducts that carried the GCR and

A station familiar to anyone who remembers the old Airfix plastic model kits, as Oakham, now thankfully restored to Rutland, was the source of the prototype Midland Railway signalbox immortalised in the kit. The box is clearly visible towards the bottom of the photograph. An empty mineral train has just passed through the station heading towards Peterborough and three cars and a cyclist wait patiently at the level crossing gates. Also clearly visible are the goods yard and track arrangements at the station.

The station is situated on the ex-Midland Railway line from Peterborough to Melton Mowbray, which opened from Stamford to Melton Mowbray on 1 May 1848.

Today, the railway continues to serve Oakham and, as can be seen the signalbox (which is a Midland Railway design dating from 1899) still stands guard over the level crossing. There has been the inevitable track rationalisation and the goods yard has gone, but otherwise the station is remarkably unchanged. **(R21542/670379)**

OSWESTRY

Then: 30 May 1966
Now: 9 September 1997

Oswestry was the headquarters of the Cambrian Railways and location of that railway's workshops. It was graced by a large station (1) as befitted its role. It was served by lines heading north to Gobowen (ex-Great Western) and by the Cambrian Railways' Whitchurch-Buttington line. The first railway to serve Oswestry was the branch from Gobowen, which opened on 23 December 1848. The first part of the future Cambrian Railways to reach Oswestry was the Oswestry & Newtown, which opened throughout on 10 June 1861

(the section from Oswestry to Pool Quay having opened on 1 May 1860). The next stage was the line from Oswestry to Whitchurch via Ellesmere; the section from Oswestry to Ellesmere opening on 27 July 1864, the section from Ellesmere to Whitchurch opening earlier the same year. It was also in July 1864 that the earlier companies were formed into the Cambrian Railways. The GWR originally had its own branch terminus serving Oswestry (2), but obtained running powers to use the new station in August 1860. The Works (3) were

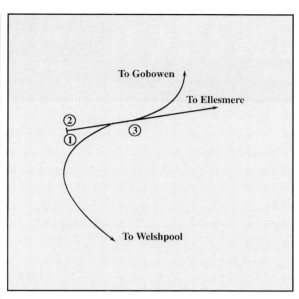

brought into use during 1866, at which time the earlier facility at Welshpool was closed. The Works handled locomotives (at the station end) and both carriages and wagons (at the Whitchurch end).

Even in the 'Then' photograph the process of rationalisation has begun. Passenger services over the line from Buttington to Whitchurch ceased on 23 November 1964 and the line from Oswestry to Ellesmere closed completely on 18 January 1965 (and is already lifted in this view). Passenger services between Gobowen and Oswestry ceased on 7 November 1966. The Works lost much of their importance after the Grouping, with much of the work being transferred to Swindon. Today, the railway remains in Oswestry (just). The freight only line linking Gobowen with the quarry at Blodwell is still extant but unused; part of the yard to the south of the station is occupied by the Cambrian Railways Society, whose long-term aim is the establishment of a preserved line over the surviving route. The grandiose station still survives as do the buildings of the former works. (**A162960/671409**)

OXFORD

Then: 1935
Now: 16 August 1997

Taken just prior to the outbreak of World War 2, this view illustrates well the close proximity between the Great Western station (1) and the LMS (ex-London & North Western) Rewley Road station (2) and goods shed (3), both of which were accessed via a swing bridge. As with Cambridge, the University authorities were initially reluctant to see the opening of a railway. However, the Oxford Railway, which was supported by the GWR, opened its line from Didcot to a station south of the area illustrated here on 12 June 1844. This station was to survive as a passenger station until 1852, when the line north to Banbury and the new station were opened. Rewley Road station opened on 20 May 1851 with the arrival of the Buckingham Railway. The new station was constructed in a method similar to that adopted for the contemporary Crystal Palace — using prefabricated cast-iron — pioneered by Joseph Paxton.

The ex-GWR station illustrated here was the result of a modernisation scheme of the decade prior to the outbreak of World War 1 in 1914. Amongst work carried out at this

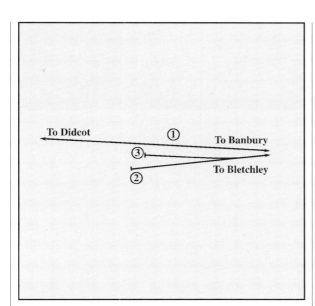

time was the extension of the down platform, the enlarging of the river bridge to the north of the station to allow access to bays at the north end and an extended platform canopy on the up platform.

The pre-World War 1 station serving the GWR lines survived until 1970 when it was replaced by a prefabricated structure, which has itself now been demolished in favour of the new station illustrated in the 'Now' photograph, which opened in May 1990. One structure that has survived throughout, however, is the platform canopy extension of 1910, which is visible at the northern end of the up platform. Adjacent to the canopy is the parcels office and bay platform from which the recently restored service to Bicester Town operates. Rewley Road station closed on 1 October 1951 when services were transferred to the ex-GWR station. The building, or at least part of it, survives. The area formerly occupied by the LNWR goods yard is now occupied by a car park and the former LNWR coal yard has also closed (the track over the swing bridge being removed in 1985). The sidings to the south of the station have also disappeared. (**47766/670331**)

PAIGNTON
(GOODRINGTON)

Then: 24 July 1965
Now: 10 October 1997

With Goodrington Sands in the foreground, it is easy to see why the Devon coast at Paignton became a popular holiday destination. The railway originally reached Paignton, courtesy of the Dartmouth & Torbay Railway on 2 August 1859. This company was absorbed by the South Devon Railway in 1862 and then by the Great Western Railway in 1878. The station serving the town is situated to the north of this photograph. The line south to Kingswear opened on 16 August 1864 (passengers) and 2 April 1866 (freight). The line south from Paignton to Goodrington was doubled in 1928, at which time the signalbox illustrated here was provided; Goodrington Halt was opened in July 1928. The carriage sidings illustrated were constructed as late as 1956/57. Note the 'Western'

class diesel-hydraulic in the up platform of the station.

Today, whilst much of the infrastructure remains intact there have been significant changes. The freight facilities at Goodrington were withdrawn in 1967 and, on 1 November 1972, operation of the Kingswear-Paignton section was transferred from British Railways to the Dart Valley Railway; it now operates under the name of the Paignton & Dartmouth Railway. The double-track section from Goodrington to Paignton is treated as two separate lines; the former up line is retained by the main line railway for continued access to the surviving carriage sidings, whilst the former down line is used by P&DR trains gaining access to their own station at Paignton. **(A151215/67213)**

Then: 12 August 1964
Now: 17 June 1998

This dramatic view, taken looking almost due north, emphasises Perth's role as the gateway to the Highlands. The centre of the photograph is dominated by Perth station, with the main line from the south approaching from the bottom of the photograph. The platforms and line serving Dundee can be seen curving sharply away to the east, whilst the main line towards Stanley Junction passes through the station and on onwards to the north. Immediately to the northwest of the station can be seen the ex-NBR goods yard; the NBR gained access to Perth via running powers from Hilton Junction to the south. Further north can be seen the extensive ex-Caledonian freight facilities at Dovecotland. Finally, in the far distance, can be determined the junction with the line to Crieff at Almond Junction. The station hotel, built in 1890 in a Scottish baronial style and jointly owned by the CR, HR and NBR, can be seen in the triangle formed by the main station and the platforms for Dundee. The main station was designed by Sir William Title in 1848, although the station was considerably enlarged in both 1884 and 1893.

The first line to serve Perth was that from Dundee, which opened on 24 May 1847; initially this line terminated on the north bank of the River Tay and it was not until 8 March 1849 that trains crossed the river at Perth and connected with the line, the Scottish Central, which had opened to Perth from the south on 22 May

1848. The future NBR line, the Edinburgh & Northern, reached Hilton Junction on 18 July 1848. This was followed on 20 August 1848 by the opening of the line from Perth to Forfar. The future Highland main line, the Perth & Dunkeld, opened north from Stanley Junction on 7 April 1856. Finally, the line from Almond Junction towards Crieff opened on 1 January 1858.

Today, Perth remains an important junction. The line from Stirling to Stanley Junction and thence to Inverness survives, although the ex-CR lines to Forfar (over which the 'A4' Pacifics ran their swansong services on Glasgow-Aberdeen expresses) have closed as has the branch towards Crieff. The line towards Dundee is also still operational. The branch to Crieff succumbed on 1 October 1951 (passengers) and — beyond the Dewars' siding at Inveralmond — on 11 September 1967 (freight). The line from Stanley Junction lost its passenger services on 4 September 1967 and closed completely on 5 June 1982. The scene today is equally dramatic, but not just for the landscape but also for the changes that have affected the railway network. Although, as elsewhere, there is contraction, one notable exception in Perth is the development of Perth Yard to the north of the city. The station retains its roof and the sharply curved platforms still provide access for the line towards Dundee. **(R21200/675381)**

PETERBOROUGH

Then: 19 July 1932
Now: 16 August 1997

This view looking east along the River Nene shows lines from four of the five companies that served this cathedral city; the exception is the Midland & Great Northern, which approached Peterborough from the north. Running parallel to the Nene is the ex-London & North Western (ex-London & Birmingham Railway) line from Northampton; this route opened on 2 June 1845 and was the first to serve the city. This line used a station, later

Peterborough East, which was owned by the Eastern Counties (later Great Eastern), which was to open to Ely to freight traffic on 10 December 1846 and to passenger services on 14 January 1847. The ex-LNWR and ex-GER lines made an end-on connection approximately where the foot crossing is located next to the ex-LNWR locomtive shed (closed on 8 February 1932). The Midland Railway route from Stamford had opened on 2 October 1846, and

this route is the coming down towards Peterborough East over the Nene on the curved alignment. The final arrival was the Great Northern, running north to south over the river through the girder bridge, which opened to Peterborough on 8 August 1850 and from Peterborough to Grantham on 1 August 1852; this line is part of the East Coast main line between London and Scotland.

Peterborough has become a new town and has seen a considerable population and commercial expansion — remember 'The Peterborough Effect'? Whilst much of the railway infrastructure survives, there have been a number of developments. The ex-LNWR line to Northampton lost its passenger services on 6 June 1966 and was subsequently closed completely; the section from

Wansford towards Peterborough was, however, preserved by the Nene Valley and a new station, Peterborough Town, was built to serve the NVR. Adjacent to the new station can be seen the stock, including an ex-Danish State Railways Pacific, gathered for the Rail World display located on the site of the now demolished shed. Peterborough East station has now closed completely, with passenger services diverted over the ex-Midland Railway line to the ex-GNR station. The East Coast main line has now been electrified and EMUs operated by West Anglia Great Northern — the newly privatised Train Operating Company — can be seen stabled in the Nene carriage sidings. (C15542/670349)

PLYMOUTH

Then: 22 September 1961
Now: 10 October 1997

The 'Then' shot is noted by Aerofilms as 'New bridge at Laira' and it shows clearly the construction work involved in the rebuilding of the A379 bridge over the River Plym. For railway enthusiasts, however, there is also much of interest. Adjacent to the road bridge is the ex-London & South Western railway bridge across the river (1) that provided a link between Plymouth and Plymstock. At Plymstock, further to the southeast, the LSWR route continued to Turnchapel and the Great Western branch headed off towards Yealmpton. This ex-GWR route was completely segregated from the rest of the GWR network and was only accessed via the LSWR at this point. The ex-LSWR line can be seen heading towards Cattewater Harbour (2) underneath both the old and new road bridges, whilst Cattewater Junction (3) has already been reduced in significance with the closure and removal of the ex-GWR line to Mount Gould Junction (4). At Friary Junction (5), Where the London & South Western met the GWR — like the GWR's Yealmpton branch — the LSWR's approaches

to its station at Plymouth Friary were isolated from the rest of the company's lines — the GWR headed southwards (6) towards Sutton Harbour. Finally, the approaches to the LSWR's Friary station can be seen (7).

The earliest railway alignment in this view predates the arrival of the main line companies; the 4ft 6in gauge Plymouth & Dartmoor was opened from Sutton Pool to King Tor on 26 September 1823. The broad gauge line serving Sutton Harbour, which opened in May 1853, ran alongside the earlier line, which was closed in 1869. The first incursion by the LSWR came with the opening of the line to Cattewater on 3 August 1880, but the major expansion came with the opening of the line to the new terminus at Friary on 1 July 1891. This was followed by the opening of the line across the River Plym to Plymstock on 5 September 1892. The LSWR branch was extended to Turnchapel on 1 January 1897. The GWR route from Plymstock to Yealmpton opened on 17 January 1898. Both these branches had lost their passenger

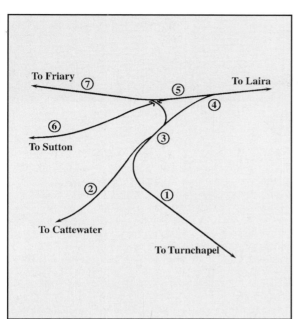

To Friary ⑦   To Laira

⑤

④

⑥

③

To Sutton

②   ①

To Cattewater

To Turnchapel

services by the date of the 'Then' photograph: those to Yealmpton were finally withdrawn on 6 October 1947 and those to Turnchapel on 10 September 1951. Freight over the Yealmpton branch followed on 29 February 1960 and those beyond Plymstock to the Admiralty Wharves at Turnchapel succumbed less than a fortnight after the date of the 'Then' photograph (on 2 October 1961). Also by the date of the 'Then' photograph, Plymouth Friary had lost its remaining passenger services (on 15 September 1958) as, under the Modernisation Plan, it was to become Plymouth's primary freight yard.

Today, the scene is recognisable, although over the past 36 years there have been further reductions in the railway operation. Whilst the bridge across the Plym remains, the last freight traffic across it (to a cement terminal at Plymstock) was withdrawn on 10 February 1989. The Sutton Harbour branch was cut short of its original terminus on 18 December 1972 and was closed completely beyond Friary Junction on 3 December 1973. There remains freight traffic, however, along the remains of the Cattewater branch and the route to Plymouth Friary also remains operational. The alignment of the Sutton Harbour branch has been converted into a road but elsewhere there are still signs of continuity. (**A96507/672180**)

PRESTON

Then: 28 July 1948
Now: 8 August 1997

Located on the River Ribble, Preston is one of the most important railway junctions of the region. Apart from the West Coast main line, which runs almost due north-south through the town, Preston also saw the Lancashire & Yorkshire routes radiating out towards Blackburn, Southport and Liverpool as well as the L&YR/LNWR joint line towards Blackpool and Fleetwood and the joint branch to Longridge. Inevitably, to handle the traffic, a significant station was built at Preston, and the 'Then' view shows this station in the early days of Nationalisation. The station as illustrated was the result of major rebuilding in 1880, 1903 and 1913, by which time it had 15 platform faces; the three main island platforms, with their bays, were jointly owned, but the East Lancashire platforms, on the east side of the station, were owned by the L&YR. Apart from the main station itself,

also visible on the west side of the line — this is a view looking due north — is the ex-LNWR Christian Road goods yard; between it and the station the Ribble branch curves away to the west to Preston Dock. On the east side, adjacent to the East Lancashire platforms, is the ex-L&YR Butler Street goods yard with its warehouses. The large signalbox in the foreground is Preston No 1, whilst the foreground is dominated by the imposing bulk of the Park Hotel (jointly owned by the L&YR and LNWR), which was linked (via a covered way and footbridge) to the south end of the station.

The North Union Railway, one of the forerunners to the LNWR, reached Preston from the south on 31 October 1838; it opened its station on the present site at the same time and this small station was to be sufficient until the completion of the first rebuilding in 1880. The West Coast

main line northwards was opened on 26 June 1840. The line from Preston to Fleetwood was opened on 16 July 1840 and the Ribble branch followed on 16 July 1846. The future L&YR line reached the town with the opening of the Blackburn & Preston Railway on 1 June 1846.

Preston remains an important junction on the modern West Coast main line, although, as can be seen, the station has been much reduced. The former East Lancashire platforms have been swept away along with the Bamber Bridge-Preston station extension line (which opened on 2 September 1850 and closed on 1 May 1972) when services were rerouted via the Farington curve into the main station. Electric services between Weaver Junction and Preston were introduced on 23 July 1973 and these were extended to Glasgow on 7 May 1974. The goods yards at Christian Road and Butler Street have been swept away, the latter, along with the site of the East Lancashire platforms, now incorporated into a large car park. The Ribble branch is still extant, although it is currently out of use; a stop board was erected in April 1995 effectively severing the line. Sidings remain north of Preston station serving Dock Street depot and part of the Christian Road yard has been incorporated into a Post Office facility. **(A17822/670564)**

READING

Then: 3 August 1962
Now: 15 August 1997

This view looking northeastwards, shows the approaches to Reading General station from the west. In the foreground the lines from Basingstoke and Newbury (1) approach from Reading West station and meet the main line from Didcot (2) at West Main signalbox (3). The ex-GWR locomotive shed (coded 81D; 4) is situated in the triangle formed by the lines to the west of the station. To the north of Reading General station (5) is the Caversham Road signal works (6), whilst to the south of the station is the ex-Southern Reading South station (7). To the north and east of the signal works are the extensive ex-GWR goods facilities (8) constructed in 1896.

The first railway to serve Reading was the Great Western from Twyford, which opened on 30 March 1840. This line was extended from Reading to Steventon on 1 June 1840. The GWR line from Reading to Hungerford opened on 21 December 1848 and the triangle to the west

of Reading was completed with the West Junction-Oxford Road Junction chord on 22 December 1856. The Southern arrived, courtesy of the South Eastern Railway, on 4 July 1849 with the opening of the line from Farnborough; another constituent of the Southern, the London & South Western, reached the town via running powers over the SER from Wokingham on 9 July 1856. The first station at South was opened in 1855, but was rebuilt later that decade and was further extended, with the addition of further platforms, in the 1890s. General station dates back to the arrival of the GWR in 1840, although the buildings that survive in the 'Then' photograph postdate that era. The main station block dates to 1868 and the station was dramatically extended during the 1890s with additional platforms; it only became 'General', however, in 1949. It was proposed in the 1955 Modernisation Plan that General be rebuilt, but lack of resources mean that this project was

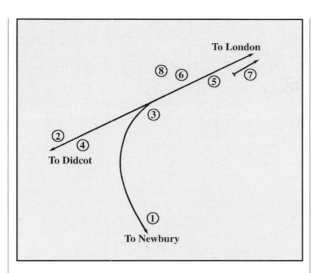

To London

⑧ ⑥ ⑤ ⑦

③

② ④

To Didcot

①

To Newbury

not progressed; Reading had to wait more than 30 years for a major rebuild. The signal works at Reading dated back to 1859 although the site was modernised, after a fire, with work being completed in March 1952. The first GWR locomotive shed at Reading was opened in November 1840 adjacent to the station; the shed as illustrated here dates from a relocation in 1880 and subsequent rebuilding culminating in a conversion from a roundhouse to a nine-road straight shed in the early 1930s.

Today, Reading remains one of the most important stations serving express and local services through the Thames Valley. Reading General (now called simply Reading again) saw a major rebuilding project, which was opened by HM The Queen on 4 April 1989; this work included the construction of a new overbridge at the eastern end of the station and new concourse area with retail outlets. All passenger services have been concentrated into the ex-GWR station; Reading South closed on 4 September 1965 after which services were transferred to new platforms (Nos 4A/4B) at General. The site of Reading South has been swallowed up by redevelopment. The locomotive shed lost its steam allocation in January 1965 and the old steam shed was demolished soon afterwards, but the diesel maintenance depot (constructed in 1959 but out of view in the 'Then' photograph) remained. The DMU shed was extended in the early 1960s to provide maintenance facilities for main line locomotives. Reading received a new power signalbox in 1965 and this allowed for the closure of mechanical signalboxes, such as Reading Main Line West, from 26 April 1965; the power box can just be seen to the north of the station in the 'Now' photograph. In order to release the land for redevelopment, the signal works was to be transferred; the site at Caversham Road closed on 29 June 1984. On a more positive note, the introduction to service of the new Thames Turbos in the early 1990s saw the opening of a new maintenance depot alongside the line towards Reading West. **(A106932/670462)**

RYDE ST JOHNS ROAD
(ISLE OF WIGHT)

Then: 20 July 1954
Now: 17 November 1997

Located on the line from Ryde Pier to Ventnor, Ryde was (and is) a major centre on the small Isle of Wight railway network. The line from St John's Road to Shanklin was opened on 23 August 1864 by the Isle of Wight Eastern Section Railway Co (later the Isle of Wight Railway). The section north from St John's Road to the Pier Head was constructed for the London & South Western Railway and the London Brighton & South Coast Railway. It opened in two stages: from St John's Road to Esplanade on 5 April 1880 and thence to Pier Head on 12 July 1880. It was at Ryde that the Isle of Wight Railway had its small workshops and shed, both of which are visible here. In the 'Then' shot a tank engine is ready to depart with a passenger service, whilst adjacent to the locomotive shed

can be seen a further three of the ubiquitous 'O2' class 0-4-4Ts. Ryde shed was classified 71F until 1954, when it became 70H until its final closure in March 1967.

By 1997, although there has been some rationalisation — most notably with the loss of the shed — the station survives as does the locomotive works which now services the second-generation ex-London Underground EMUs that operate the route between Pier Head and Shanklin. In this view it possible to see six of the two car sets. At the time of writing these were still painted in Network SouthEast livery; how long will it be before the new privatised operators of the line, Island Line (a subsidiary of Stagecoach), repaint the stock in that operator's livery? **(R21067/672822)**

ST IVES
(CORNWALL)

Then: 7 July 1946
Now: 10 October 1997

St Ives, situated on the north Cornish coast, has long been a popular holiday destination — clearly evident here by the numbers on the beach in the foreground. The branch from St Erth, some four miles long, was built by the West Cornwall Railway and opened on 1 June 1877. It was the last broad gauge branch to be built. The WCR was incorporated into the Great Western Railway on 1 August 1878. The branch was converted to standard gauge in May 1892. As can be seen the station was provided with a single platform with bay and run round loops, a goods shed and a single-road engine shed.

The branch from St Erth to St Ives survives today — although being threatened with closure in the Beeching Report (and consequently featuring in the classic Michael Flanders and Donald Swann song 'Slow Train') — albeit in a much reduced state. The engine shed was closed in September 1961, although the track was not removed for a further two years. The track serving the goods yard and run round loop was removed in early 1966. Finally, on 23 May 1971, the line was slightly foreshortened to serve a new single platform; the area occupied being adapted to form an enlarged car park. **(7152/672190)**

SHEFFIELD

Then: 19 June 1961
Now: 4 September 1997

This view, looking north to south, shows the relationship between the Midland and Great Central lines in the steel city. On the extreme right is Sheffield Victoria station with the electrified line heading westwards over the Midland main line. The Midland main line heads southwards towards Sheffield Midland station. In the foreground are the platforms of Attercliffe Road station. Alongside Victoria station is the ex-GCR Park goods yard, whilst also visible, at the extreme top of the photograph is the ex-London & North Western Wharf Street goods yard. Running from the Midland main line at Nunnery Main Line Junction to the ex-GCR line is the ex-MR spur that provided a link between the two routes, over which (after modification in 1965) services from the Retford and Penistone directions were gradually diverted into Sheffield Midland station leading to the eventual closure of Victoria station. At Nunnery were located carriage sidings. The ex-GCR route across the Pennines, from Sheffield to

Manchester, was electrified in the early 1950s; the section from Sheffield to Penistone being energised at 1,500V dc on 20 September 1954.

The future Great Central line opened from Dunford Bridge to Sheffield (Bridgehouses) on 14 July 1845 and was extended from Bridgehouses to Woodhouse Junction on 12 February 1849. Sheffield Victoria opened on 15 September 1851, at which time the original station at Bridgehouses closed. The Park goods line opened in September 1854. The section of the Midland main line illustrated here, from Grimesthorpe Junction to Chesterfield (via Sheffield Midland), opened on 1 February 1870; the original MR station serving Sheffield, Wicker, was located slightly to the north of Victoria and closed when the new route opened. The link line, owned by the Midland, between the ex-GC and ex-MR lines at Nunnery, opened for goods traffic in August 1870; it did not carry passenger services until the completion of the modifications in 1965; and passenger services first used the route on 4 October 1965. The LNWR goods yard and line at Wharf Street opened on 2 February 1903; the yard was known as City until 25 September 1950.

The ex-GCR Park goods yard closed on 1 June 1963; this was followed on 12 July 1965 by the closure of the former LNWR goods yard at Wharf Street. From late 1965 passenger services from the Retford direction were diverted into Midland station. Through passenger services between Victoria and Manchester were withdrawn on 5 January 1970 at which time Victoria was closed; passenger services, however, continued to pass through the station from Huddersfield *en route* to reversal at Nunnery for access to Midland. This continued until 16 May 1983 when the surviving services were diverted to run via Barnsley. This allowed for the complete closure of the former GC route between Deepcar and Penistone. Today, the scene is recognisable. The ex-MR main line from Rotherham still bisects the picture from north to south and the curve to Nunnery is still operational. Sheffield Victoria is, however, a part of history, although a freight line still runs past the site *en route* to Deepcar. Attercliffe Road station is now closed. More positive is the presence of the Sheffield Supertram network and the route running into the city centre can be seen crossing over the ex-MR main line. (**A91310/671603**)

SHREWSBURY

Then: 18 July 1961
Now: 9 September 1997

Few stations in Britain can have a more dramatic location than that serving Shrewsbury. With its platforms straddling the River Severn and with the site overshadowed by the remains of Shrewsbury Castle, the station is a fitting monument to the panache of the Victorian railway engineers. The 'Then' photograph shows the extent of the railway facilities serving the town prior to the loss of the station's overall roof. Visible beyond the Abbey (today famous as the home of the fictional Brother Cadfael) lies the Abbey station (1) of the Shropshire & Montgomery Railway; by this date passenger services had ceased, but the site remained operational as a freight terminal. On the line heading towards Wellington is Abbey Foregate goods (2), whilst adjacent to the station is the ex-LNWR Shropshire Union Yard (3) and the Howard Street warehouse (4; originally built as the Butter Market in 1836). On the route southwards towards Hereford can be seen Coleham locomotive shed (5; which served both

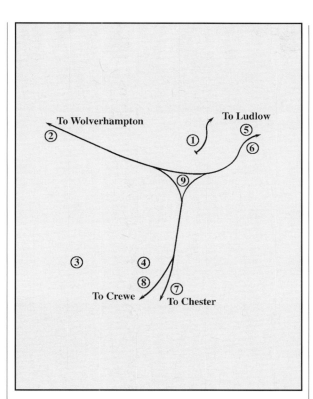

GWR and LNWR locomotives) and Coleham goods (6). To the north of the station can be seen the lines for Chester (7) and Crewe (8), whilst at the south end of the station is the now famous Severn Bridge Junction signalbox (9). Shrewsbury station was GW/LNWR joint and, as illustrated here, dated from a major enlargement undertaken at the turn of the century. Until 1924 there was also an overall roof at the north end of the station; the actual station buildings were enlarged in 1901 when a new ground floor was excavated under the existing structure.

In the 1990s, Shrewsbury remains a major railway crossroads, with lines heading to Chester, Crewe, Wolverhampton, Hereford and the Cambrian Coast. The station survives, although the overall roof was removed in the early 1960s. Elsewhere there have been great changes. The remaining freight traffic to Abbey station ceased in the late 1980s and the site has been cleared; the old S&M platform, however, survives as part of a footpath. The freight yards at Coleham (15 August 1966), Abbey Foregate (10 October 1968) and Shropshire Union (5 April 1971) have all closed, although carriage sidings remain at Abbey Foregate. Coleham shed has also closed and the buildings have been demolished. A new conveyor linking the station with the GPO sorting office was opened in the early 1960s; this is visible at the northern end of the station. Shrewsbury remains a haven of semaphore signalling and a prominent survivor is the box at Severn Bridge Junction; this 1903 LNWR-built structure is now the largest mechanical box on BR. (A93735/671546)

SOUTHAMPTON

Then: 17 July 1967
Now: 11 November 1997

Viewed looking northwards, the approaches to Southampton Terminus station (1) can be seen from Northam. However, the scene is dominated by the dock and harbour facilities provided at the confluence of the rivers Itchen and Test. The Itchen approaches from the north and the famous 'Floating Bridge' can be seen (2) adjacent to the Outer Dock (1843; 3). By this date, the Inner Dock (1851; 4) had already been abandoned and filled in. Adjacent to the Inner Dock is Empress Yard (5) which was alongside the Empress Dock (1890; 6). The Ocean Dock (1911; 7) was provided with the famous Ocean Terminal (8) in 1953; boat trains, connecting with the transatlantic liners, ran from the terminal to London Waterloo. Two passenger lines are visible, one clearly undergoing maintenance in a drydock. Further west can be seen the Town Quay (9) whilst on the east bank of the Itchen can be seen the St Denys-Fareham railway line (10). By the date of this photograph, Southampton

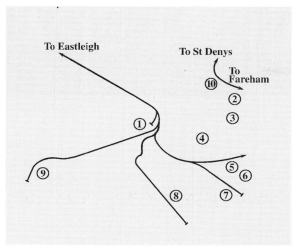

To Eastleigh

To St Denys

To Fareham

① ② ③ ④ ⑤ ⑥ ⑦ ⑧ ⑨ ⑩

opened its line from Southampton to Winchester on 10 June 1839. The station at Southampton — the future Terminus — had a facade designed by Sir William Tite. The route from Northam, through Southampton Central towards the west (the present day passenger route) dates from 1847. The primary attraction of Southampton was that it possessed a port which could be accessed at all states of the tide; the docks illustrated here were acquired by the LSWR in 1892 and the growth in the transatlantic maritime business continued. It was from Southampton that the ill-fated *Titanic* set sail in 1912; the building of the Ocean Dock in 1911 was a reflection of the growth of the trade.

Today, Terminus station is closed, but a line continues to run from Northam to the Associated British Ports facility at Southampton. Occasional passenger workings to link in with liners operate, although the Ocean Terminal was controversially demolished. The Town Quay lost its rail connections on 4 May 1980. The Floating Bridge has been replaced by a new, fixed, structure. The drydock illustrated in the 'Then' photograph has been partially infilled, whilst the Outer Dock and Town Quay show evidence in the boom in leisure sailing.
(A174654/672817)

Terminus had already lost its passenger services; the station was closed on 5 September 1966.

The London & Southampton Railway (later a major constituent of the London & South Western Railway)

SOUTHEND-ON-SEA

Then: 22 March 1968
Now: 2 September 1997

The coastal Essex town of Southend-on-Sea was served by both the Great Eastern and London, Tilbury & Southend railways. By the date of the 'Then' photograph both routes had been electrified. In the foreground, running from west to east, is the ex-LT&SR line serving Southend Central; East station is slightly off the photograph to the right. The LT&SR line reached Southend on 1 March 1856 and Central was the line's terminus until the extension eastwards to Shoeburyness was opened on 1 February

1884. To the north of Central station is the ex-GER Southend Victoria station, which was served by a branch running from Shenfield. The Great Eastern reached Southend with the opening of the line on 1 October 1889. The Shenfield-Victoria line was electrified from 31 December 1956 at 1,500V dc; (it was converted to 6.25kV in 1960) and later to 25kV (1980). The ex-LT&SR line was electrified at 25kV — except for sections between Leigh and Shoeburyness and from Barking to

Fenchurch Street which were to be at 6.25kV — with full services commencing on 18 June 1962 (limited services had started on 6 November 1961).

Some 30 years on, Southend is still served by Central and Victoria stations; unlike the scene in the late 1960s, however, competition has returned with two of the new Train Operating Companies — Great Eastern at Victoria and LTS Rail at Central — providing electric services to Liverpool Street and Fenchurch Street respectively. Although the railway scene has not changed dramatically, elsewhere there are significant changes with considerable redevelopment. **(A178480/670694)**

SOUTH SHIELDS

Then: 11 October 1950
Now: 23 October 1997

This view, taken looking almost due north, shows the railway infrastructure at South Shields with the River Tyne visible at the top left of the photograph. With its curved trainshed roof, South Shields station was rebuilt in 1879; its designer was probably William Peachey, who was employed by the North Eastern Railway in 1876/77. The North Eastern Railway route can be seen heading southeastwards past one of the numerous coal-related sites of the region. Stabled on the right of the photograph is a rake of Tyneside electric stock. Although the NER had electrified suburban routes north of the Tyne prior to the Grouping, it was left to the LNER to undertake electrification south of the Tyne; the route from Newcastle Central to South Shields being converted throughout on 14 March 1938. The chosen method of electrification was 600V dc and evidence of the third-rail can be clearly seen.

The rolling stock illustrated is that built by the NER at York Works in 1920 for the north Tyne services, which were transferred south of the river in 1938.

Taking as its reference point the still extant gasometer, it is clear that there have been a number of changes at South Shields. Firstly, there is now no evidence of the once thriving coal industry. Secondly, the original BR main line from South Shields has disappeared in favour of a new alignment used by the replacement Tyne & Wear Metro units. BR passenger services, by this date diesel-operated rather than electric, were withdrawn on 1 June 1981, at which time the original alignment between Harton Junction and South Shields was closed completely. The new Metro service approaches the station, which has also been demolished and replaced with a new single-track structure with carriage sidings beyond, over an elevated section closer to the town centre into which the original carriage sidings, on which the EMU is situated in the 'Then' photograph, have been incorporated. **(R13909/672617)**

STAFFORD

Then: 31 July 1957
Now: 9 September 1997

Served by the London & North Western and the Great Northern railways, Stafford was, and is, an important junction for West Coast services. Pictured in the 'Then' photograph before electrification, the ex-GNR route towards Uttoxeter (1) heads off to the north. Also visible is the ex-GNR Doxey Road goods depot (2). Stafford station (3) served both LNWR and GNR trains, although it was owned by the former. The LNWR route towards Norton Bridge heads off northwestwards (4), whilst the ex-LNWR line towards Shrewsbury can be seen diverging to the southwest (5). Trent Valley Junction, where the LNWR lines towards Colwich and Wolverhampton split, and the LNWR goods yard is based, are situated to the south of the station (6). The first railway through Stafford was the Grand Junction, which opened from Birmingham to Warrington via Wolverhampton and Stafford on 4 July 1837. This was followed on 15 September 1847 by the

Trent Valley line from Rugby through Colwich to Stafford and on 1 June 1849 by the branch to Wellington. The last arrival was the Stafford & Uttoxeter, which opened in 1881. The S&U line had, even by the date of the 'Then' photograph, seen passenger services withdrawn (on 4 September 1939) and closure north from Stafford Common Air Ministry (16MU) Sidings on 5 March 1951. The track was, however, still intact in 1957 and the last train, an SLS special, ran over the route in that year. The Stafford works of the famous locomotive builder W. G. Bagnall Ltd are also visible (8); the company was taken over by English Electric in 1961 and locomotive construction ended at the works in 1962.

In the 40 years since the 'Then' photograph was taken, Stafford has seen further changes. The Stafford-Wellington line lost its passenger services on 7 September 1964 and was closed completely between Stafford and Newport on

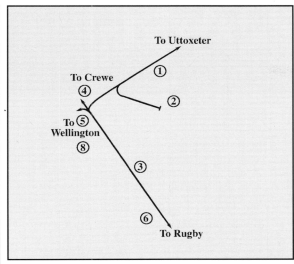

1 August 1966 (although a stub at the Stafford end still serves an industrial site). The major change came with the electrification of the West Coast main line. The line from Crewe to Stafford was electrified at 25kV from 7 January 1963 and thence to Lichfield on 22 October 1963. The line from Stafford to Wolverhampton followed on 18 April 1966. The ex-GNR goods yard at Doxey Road received a new lease of life as a base for engineering trains during the electrification process; this role was, however, not to last long and the remains of the GNR route were closed in December 1975. At the same time as the route was electrified, a new station was built at Stafford; this opened in 1964 and replaced the ex-LNWR station dating from 1861 illustrated in the 'Then' photograph. Today, although both routes are long closed, it is still possible to identify the trackbeds of the routes towards Uttoxéter and Wellington. South of the station are visible sidings used by the civil engineers, whilst the West Coast main line stretches into the distance northwestwards. (**A68598/671374**)

STEVENAGE

Then: 17 April 1967
Now: 18 November 1997

The Great Northern Railway opened through Stevenage on 7 August 1850 and this illustration shows the station in its original location. As can be seen, there is considerable construction work in the immediate vicinity. This was a reflection of the fact that Stevenage had been designated one of five new towns under the 1946 New Towns Act, with the result that its population increased from 6,625 in 1951 to some 150,000 over the next 30 years. The station illustrated in the 'Then' photograph was to be closed on 23 July 1973, when it was replaced by a new station,

situated one mile further south, which serves the town today. As can be seen, there is now little trace of the original station on the electrified East Coast main line at this point. Electrification of the Great Northern suburban services brought 25kV EMUs to Stevenage in the late 1970s and the subsequent electrification of the East Coast main line northwards to the West Riding, the northeast and Scotland now means that the route sees Class 91 electric locomotives with rakes of Mark 4 coaches. **(A170168/672855)**

STOCKTON-ON-TEES

Then: 3 September 1949
Now: 22 October 1997

There are few names more redolent of railway history than Stockton; it was, after all, one half of that most famous of railways — the Stockton & Darlington. And yet, there are perhaps few locations more indicative of the decline of both the railway industry in Britain as well as the disappearance of the once traditional heavy industries than this location. This view, looking northeastwards, shows in the foreground Bowesfield Junction, with a freight train having come round the curve from Stockton station itself via Hartburn Junction. Another train can be seen coming in from the Shildon direction, whilst the main line also heads southwards towards Stockton Cut Junction and Eaglescliffe. The lines to the east head off towards Middlesbrough along the south bank of the River Tees — the bridge across the river is out of picture on the right — whilst the extensive freight facilities provided on the line between Bowesfield Junction and the River Tees are clearly delineated.

The Stockton & Darlington Railway opened its main line to a wharf on the River Tees on 27 September 1825. The original S&DR passenger terminus was on the section of line between Bowesfield Junction and the river; this was, however, cut back towards the junction and on 1 July 1848 passenger services were transferred to Stockton South (later Thornaby) station leaving the original route to be freight only. The S&DR's Middlesbrough extension was opened on 27 December 1830; the original means across the Tees at this point was a suspension bridge but this was unsuccessful and was replaced by a stone and cast-iron bridge in 1841. The alignment of the S&DR south of Stockton to Eaglescliffe was modified in 1852/53 by the arrival of the Leeds Northern.

The dramatic change over the past 50 years is all too evident here. Although the lines from Middlesbrough to Stockton and to Eaglescliffe remain, the once extensive facilities at Bowesfield Junction have been much reduced. The line towards Shildon was closed completely on 3 July 1967. The freight service on the Bowesfield Junction-Stockton South goods line continued until complete closure on 28 June 1985. The slightly wider view of the 'Now' photograph allows for a view of the railway bridge across the Tees; this was rebuilt in the early 20th century, albeit using the foundations and masonry from the 1841 bridge. Also all too evident is the disappearance of much of the local industry. Alongside the railway is now the A66(T) road linking Middlesbrough with Darlington and the A1. **(C19470/672646)**

STOKE-ON-TRENT

Then: 6 July 1961
Now: 7 August 1997

Situated at the heart of the Potteries, Stoke-on-Trent is an amalgamation, not of five towns, as portrayed by the novelist Arnold Bennett, but of six. Evidence of the staple industry of the region can be found in the clay pits seen in this view looking southwards. Stoke station can be seen with its overall roof, whilst in the distance the approaches for the junction of the lines towards Leek and Derby are visible. The Trent & Mersey Canal is visible alongside the railway. The station buildings were designed by H. A. Hunt, a London architect, in 1850 as part of the laying out of Winton Square; he was also responsible for the North Stafford Hotel directly opposite the station, which also dates to 1850. The overall roof was constructed in 1893.

The North Staffordshire Railway first served Stoke when it opened the line from Norton Bridge (on 3 April 1848 to goods traffic and 17 April to passenger services). This was

followed by the opening of the line to Uttoxeter on 7 August 1848 and that to Crewe on 9 October 1848. Later lines saw Stoke linked to Market Drayton (via Silverdale) and to Leek; all these routes were operated by the NSR.

Today Stoke is served by electric trains over the West Coast main line and by DMUs operating between Crewe and Derby. As can be seen the 1850 station and environs as well as the 1893 trainshed are largely unchanged, although the catenary associated with the 25kV electrification is evident. The goods facilities to the west of the station have gone and the trackwork has been considerably rationalised. Electric services over the route

through Stoke were introduced on 5 December 1966. The slightly wider angle of the 'Now' photograph allows a view, in the distance, of the point where the line towards Uttoxeter diverges from the WCML; Also at that point can be seen the line heading towards Leek; passenger services over the route to Leek ceased on 7 May 1956, but the line was retained for freight, primarily to terminals at Caldon and Oakamoor. This traffic has now ceased and the line from Stoke is 'mothballed'; the far end of the Oakamoor line is now being preserved as the modern North Staffordshire Railway, based at Cheddleton. **(A92512/670584)**

STRATFORD

Then: 8 May 1963
Now: 1 October 1997

This view, taken looking southwestwards, shows the approaches to Stratford from the east. In the foreground is Maryland station (which opened originally in 1873 as Maryland Point and was rebuilt in 1946 as part of the Shenfield electrification scheme; 1). Beyond the goods yard (2) can be seen Stratford station (3). Immediately to the east of the station a line (4) can be seen curving to the south; it will connect in to the route towards North Woolwich at Sheet Factory Junction. From Stratford station the line curves northwards towards Chobham Farm Junction; this route provided access to Temple Mills Yard (and thence towards Cambridge) and, until the conversion of the line to form an extension of the Central Line of London Underground, also the route towards Epping. Stratford shed (30A) is visible at the top of the photograph (5); this was one of the Eastern Region's

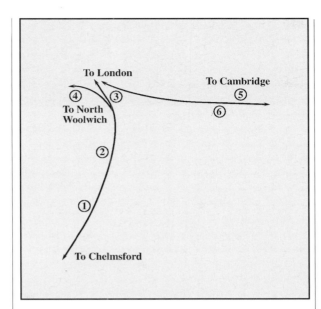

based and where many of that company's steam locomotives were built.

The first route to serve the district was the Eastern Counties Railway (later part of the Great Eastern) which opened between Devonshire Street and Romford on 18 June 1839. The route from the north opened on 15 September 1840. The North Woolwich route followed on 14 June 1847. The workshops opened in 1847/48.

Today the scene has changed a great deal. Maryland station is largely unchanged, but the Stratford area has altered considerably. The link between the GER main line and the North Woolwich line has closed, as has the goods yard. Although not readily identifiable in the photograph, a new operator — the Docklands Light Railway — now serves Stratford, running parallel to the GER main line from the west. The old locomotives works, which closed in September 1963, have been demolished, whilst the locomotive depot has been much reduced in status. Originally one of the most important heavy maintenance depots handling modern traction, the depot is currently scheduled for closure during 1998. Also gone are the carriage sidings, although a freightliner terminal has been established to the north of the locomotive depot. The slightly wider angle allows for a view of the line heading in from Dalston via Lea Junction and Channelsea North and South junctions over which the services between Richmond and Woolwich operate. The triangular junction to the west of Stratford, which provides a link between the GER main line and the route towards Dalston is also visible. (**A111030/672010**)

primary steam sheds, having an allocation of some 383 steam locomotives in 1950. However, by the date of the 'Then' photograph, steam operation from Stratford had already ceased (as from September 1962), although it remained as a base for the replacement diesel-electrics. Closer to the camera (6) is Stratford locomotive works, where the Great Eastern's locomotive department was

SUNDERLAND

Then: 23 September 1964
Now: 23 October 1997

This view, looking north towards the River Wear, shows in detail the position of Sunderland station. In the background the line crosses the Wear *en route* to Monkwearmouth and on to Newcastle, whilst in the foreground is the junction between the line towards Ryhope and Hartlepool (heading southeastwards) and that towards Penshaw (heading southwestwards). The first true railway to serve Sunderland was the Durham & Sunderland, which opened to a terminus at South Dock in 1836. The second railway, the Brandling Junction, served the north side of the Wear, opening to Monkwearmouth on 19 June 1836; the later Monkwearmouth station (now a museum) opened in 1848. The line westwards to Penshaw opened on 1 June 1853 for passenger services. The

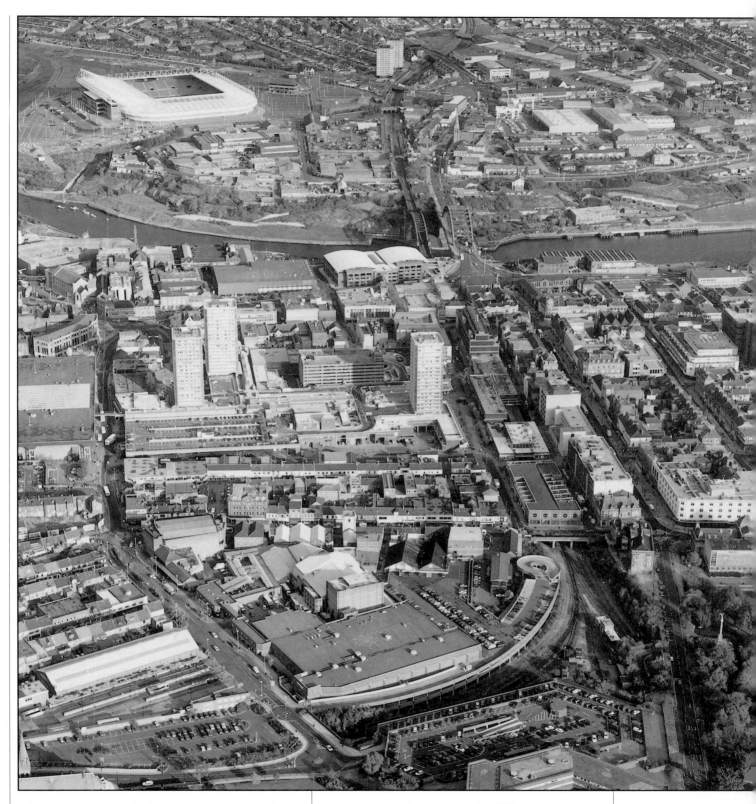

railways north and south of the river were connected on 4 August 1879, when the existing station site replaced earlier stations. The station illustrated in the 'Then' photograph was undergoing rebuilding at the time following damage during World War 2.

With the demise of the traditional heavy industries of the region — coal and shipbuilding largely disappearing from the Wear — Sunderland is now served by a passenger line from Newcastle towards Hartlepool and Tees-side. As can be seen, the mid-1960s station has been replaced with a development above. The track has been rationalised, with the link towards the Penshaw line retained only as carriage sidings. North of the river, the huge new Sunderland football stadium, named the 'Stadium of Light', was completed for the start of the 1997/98 season and was built on land reclaimed from the former Monkwearmouth colliery. (**A140609/672626**)

SWANSEA

Then: 1 September 1959
Now: 15 August 1997

As befitted one of the major industrial and maritime centres of Wales, Swansea had a particularly complex railway network, with lines inherited from three pre-Grouping companies — the Midland, the Great Western and the London & North Western. This view shows the area to the west of the River Tawe and shows, largely, the facilities provided by the LNWR here and the relationship between these lines and those of the GWR. In the

foreground can be seen Swansea Victoria station (1), the ex-LNWR terminus, with its associated goods facilities. Running in from Wind Street Junction (2) is the ex-GER line that ran east across the Tawe (3) and north towards Neath (4). The GWR line formed a junction with the LNWR route just to the west of Victoria station and gained access to Wind Street goods yard (5). Running alongside the ex-GWR route, but at a slightly lower level,

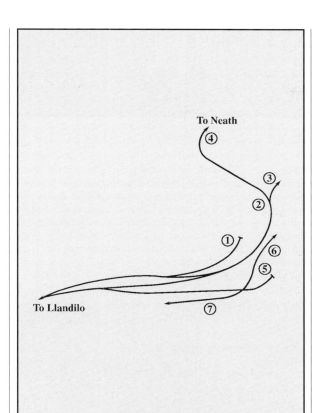

To Neath

④

③

②

①

⑥

⑤

To Llandilo

⑦

are the lines of the Swansea Harbour Trust (6), which also serve Swansea South Dock (7). Although not clearly visible, the road alongside the LNWR goods yard was the route of the Swansea & Mumbles Railways, which was, as the Oystermouth Railway, the first passenger carrying railway in the world; electrified in the 1920s, by this date the line was operated by South Wales Transport and was to close completely, early in 1960.

Taking the site of the gasometers as a reference — bottom left — the changes wrought over this part of Swansea over the past 40 years are extraordinary. The wider angle of the 'Now' shot allows for the ex-GWR terminus to be seen (top right) but of the railway infrastructure illustrated in the 'Then' view, nothing except some retaining walls in the foreground seems to survive; indeed, were it not for these odd reference points it would be difficult to imagine that this was the same scene. Passenger services into Victoria from Pontardulais were withdrawn from 15 June 1964; on the same date the line from Wind Street Junction eastwards was closed completely. These closures were followed on 4 October 1965 by the withdrawal of freight traffic over the ex-LNWR lines serving Victoria and South Dock. Finally, on 1 November 1965, the ex-GWR line from High Street via Wind Street Junction to Victoria was closed completely. **(A78437/670469)**

SWINDON

Then: 27 April 1954
Now: 11 November 1997

Swindon was another of the towns that grew rapidly with the arrival of the railways; it was the location of the Great Western Railway's main locomotive, carriage and wagon workshops and this view, taken in the 1950s, shows the great extent of the carriage and wagon works in the period. Swindon station (1) is located on the south side of the main part of the complex with the ex-GWR main line running from Didcot in the east towards Bristol. A six-coach train arriving from the Gloucester direction can be seen (2) as can the easternmost part of the locomotive works (3). However, the scene is dominated by the carriage and wagon facility; buildings visible include the carriage body and paint repair shops (4), the carriage lifting shops (5) and the wagon building and repair shops (6). On the south side of the main line the carriage works continues with the trimming shed (7), the finishing shed and the carriage body building shed (8). Also visible (9) is Swindon shed (coded 82C), which lost its steam allocation in November 1964.

214

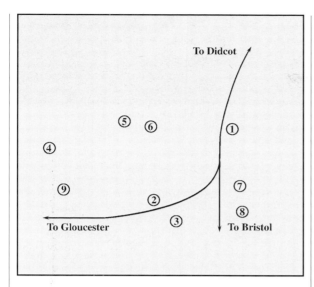

It was Daniel Gooch who argued in favour of Swindon as the location of the GWR's locomotive works and commenced operation in early 1843. It was in 1868 that the carriage works were transferred to Swindon and the site continued to grow through the 19th century. By 1892 the GWR claimed that Swindon was the largest railway works in the world, with more than 10,000 being employed. In 1948, at Nationalisation, the works covered an area of 326 acres (of which 77.5 were roofed). It was at Swindon, in 1960, that the last steam locomotive built for British Railways, No 92220 *Evening Star*, was completed.

However, as is all too evident from the 'Now' photograph, Swindon's glory days as a railway manufacturing centre have long gone. Although odd buildings, such as the carriage body and repair shops, survive, they are no longer in railway use. Swindon continues to act as a junction between the London-Bristol main line and the route to Gloucester, but the station has been rationalised and rebuilt (albeit retaining earlier platform buildings), reduced now to one island platform with bays at the western end. Contraction of the workshop area was foreshadowed in the *Main Workshops Future Plan* of 1962 which argued for the closure of almost half of BR's 31 major workshops. Carriage building ceased at Swindon in 1962 and the carriage and wagon works was closed in 1967 — repair work being transferred to the old locomotive works — and the site sold to the local council. The locomotive works passed to British Rail Engineering Ltd (BREL), but its role continued to decline; by 1975 the works occupied only 147 acres. Latterly, much of Swindon's work was in the refurbishment of EMUs. The former locomotive works was closed completely in 1985 and the site has been partially cleared, although a number of listed buildings survive. (**A53783/672845**)

TAUNTON

Then: 1939
Now: 17 November 1997

Situated on the former Bristol & Exeter section of the Great Western Railway, Taunton was first served by trains on 1 July 1842 with the opening of the Bristol & Exeter. Its importance grew with the opening on 1 October 1853 of the line from Durston to Yeovil. The first section of the branch to Minehead, from Norton Fitzwarren to Watchet, followed on 31 March 1862. Two further secondary routes followed — from Creech Junction to Chard on 11 September 1866 and from Norton Fitzwarren to

Wiveliscombe (later extended to Barnstaple) on 8 June 1871 — before the final opening, that of the shortened route to the west, which opened on 2 July 1906. The scene as illustrated here shows the station as rebuilt during the 1930s. Visible is the main station (1), the goods shed (2), the East yard (3), the engine shed (4), the East Loop signalbox (5), the goods loops running to the south (6), the West Loop signalbox (7), the West Station signalbox (8) and the West yard (9).

To Bristol

To Norton Fitzwarren

The 'Then' scene was the result of a major investment in Taunton by the GWR resulting from the fact that, by the late 1920s, the station was a major bottleneck for GWR operations. The work undertaken included the quadrupling of the running lines from Cogload Junction to Norton Fitzwarren and the complete rebuilding of the station. Work started on the latter project in September 1930 and resulted in a new station with four through roads and seven bay platforms; the new station opened on 20 December 1931. Additional work included the enlargement of the locomotive shed and, in early 1932, the doubling of the goods shed.

Today, Taunton remains an important station serving trains between the West Country and London. As can be seen, however there has been a dramatic rationalisation of facilities over the past 60 years; indeed certain activities,

such as the coal concentration depot (which existed from 1964 until 1982) do not feature in either photograph. Following closure of the lines to Barnstaple, Minehead, Chard and Yeovil, the platform facilities at Taunton were reduced. The island platform was taken out of service on 31 March 1976 and the platform buildings later demolished; the main entrance to the station was altered with the construction of a new booking office, which opened on 16 March 1983. The locomotive shed (which was coded 83B by British Railways) lost its steam allocation in 1964 and the site is now largely cleared. Rusting sidings remain both east and west of the station and the old goods yard still stands; there are, however, now no goods loops and the three signalboxes have disappeared. (**61344/672840**)

TAYPORT

Then: 27 June 1963
Now: 17 June 1998

Located on the south bank of the River Tay, in the Kingdom of Fife, Tayport was and is an important dormitory town for the city of Dundee across the river. Its railway history was to be inextricably linked with that of both the river and of Dundee. The Edinburgh & Northern Railway, later part of the North British Railway, sought to connect Dundee and Edinburgh by rail; however, its plans for a bridge across the River Tay were rejected by parliament, with the result that the company decided to

make Tayport — already linked to Broughty Ferry by boat — its terminus for services to Dundee. The line between Tayport and Leuchars, which can be seen stretching to the east in the 'Then' shot, was opened on 17 May 1850; passengers being carried by coach prior to that date. The railway had taken over the existing ferry operation in February 1846 and, on 22 July 1847, obtained powers to rebuild the harbour at Tayport; this work was completed in May 1851. The final development came with the opening

of the line between Wormit and Tayport, resulting from the opening of the first Tay Bridge; this line opened in two stages — from Wormit to Newport on 12 May 1879 and thence to Tayport on the following day.

The opening of the Tay Bridge was to have an immediate impact upon Tayport; it was no longer the terminus for services linking Edinburgh with Dundee but was the mid-point on a branch line from Wormit to Leuchars, where the majority of passenger traffic headed west, via the newer line, towards Dundee. In 1947 only some three trains a weekday operated in either direction between Tayport and Leuchars, whilst the number from Tayport towards Wormit was more than five times that number. It came as no surprise, therefore, that passenger services between Leuchars and Tayport were withdrawn on 9 January 1956, at which time the section between Leuchars and Spinning Mill Siding at Tayport was closed completely. Examining the 'Then' shot in detail, the track has been lifted in the distance, although the formation remains.

It was, however, to be the opening of another bridge — the Tay road bridge — that was to prove the death-knell of the line. Passenger services were withdrawn between Wormit and Tayport on 5 May 1969. The line between Newport and Spinning Mill Siding via Tayport had lost its freight services on 23 May 1966, and the section from Newport to Wormit was to close completely on 5 May 1969.

Today, the population of Tayport has grown and new residential developments have obscured the site of the closed station. Although it is possible to see the former alignment heading off towards Leuchars in the distance, there is now no evidence in the town that it was once served by a railway. (**A115974/675373**)

Then: 12 April 1950
Now: November 1997

The Wiltshire town of Trowbridge is situated on the line between Bradford on Avon and Westbury. The ex-Great Western route was opened between Thingley and Westbury on 5 September 1848. The town was a major centre of the local woollen industry and, as can be seen, was provided with extensive goods facilities. The station was served by cross-country freight and passenger trains.

Despite the considerable freight traffic evinced in the 'Then' photograph, Trowbridge lost its freight facilities on 10 July 1967. Today the former goods yard is still in use for freight transport, but for the road rather than rail. The station buildings have been considerably rationalised and the up bay and sidings, located on the east side of the station, have been replaced by a car park. **(A28647/672814)**

TYNEMOUTH

For some 300 years the northeast of England was the source of huge quantities of coal, much of which was transferred by ship to the fuel-hungry southeast of England (in particular, London). This was the period when the cliché 'Coals to Newcastle' was coined and it was inevitable that the railways would provide a vast array of infrastructure to handle this lucrative traffic. This is the north bank of the River Tyne at Whitehill Point, Percy Main, slightly inland from North Shields and Tynemouth. Percy Mains station, on the line from Newcastle to

Tynemouth, can be seen in the distance with the line heading eastwards towards Tynemouth. A rail overbridge carries this line over the freight line from Backworth which passes under the A187 road on its way to the staithes. Further to the south of this bridge a junction provides access to the docks further west and a loop then links back into the line north towards Backworth. The origin of the line north to Backworth was the Blyth & Tyne Railway, later part of the North Eastern Railway, which was the result of coalmine owners in the Blyth area

wanting access to a deeper port than that at Blyth; the line was planned in 1843 taking over the align-ment of the earlier Seghill Railway (of 1840) and opened in 1846 for freight and on 3 March 1847 for passengers; the latter were not to last long, being withdrawn south of Backworth (Earsdon Junction) from 27 June 1864.

There is, perhaps, no greater indication as to the decline in the staple industries of northeast England than in this view. There is now no evidence whatsoever of the once lucrative coal traffic; the port area remains, but it is now used as a car ferry terminal for Scandinavia Seaways' services to the continent. The line to Percy Main North survived until 1980; the section from Percy Main North to Middle Engine Lane survives as the basis of the Stephenson Railway Museum project. **(R11784/672618)**

WAKEFIELD

Then: 16 September 1946
Now: 9 March 1998

This view, looking south, shows the eastern end of the station at Wakefield Kirkgate. The main station building can be seen in the extreme bottom right hand corner of the photograph. At the platform ends, the lines divide with one line heading southwards towards Calder Bridge Junction, visible in the distance; the line from Calder Bridge Junction heading in a northeasterly direction forms a further junction with the Wakefield-Normanton line at Turners Lane Junction.

The Calder Valley main line through Wakefield Kirkgate was opened by the Manchester & Leeds Railway (known as the Lancashire & Yorkshire after 9 July 1847) between Hebden Bridge and Goose Hill Junction, where it met the earlier York & North Midland main line into Leeds, on 5 October 1840. Although situated on the LYR main line, Kirkgate was a joint station with the Great Northern Railway from 23 August 1853. Kirkgate became a junction with the opening of the line through Oakenshaw

to Goole on 1 April 1848. The main station building at Kirkgate dates from the opening of the line although the station was significantly reconstructed in 1854 with the arrival of the GNR.

Today, Wakefield Kirkgate is very much the second station in the city; the ex-GNR Westgate station is served by the electrified trains of the East Coast route between Leeds and Doncaster. Kirkgate has seen DMU services on the Westgate-Kirkgate (reverse)-Huddersfield line and from Barnsley towards Leeds. The line southwards towards Canal Bridge Junction saw its passenger services withdrawn on 2 January 1967, but these were reinstated to provide a link with Pontefract Monkhill in the early 1990s,

and the line also provides access, *inter alia*, to the remaining freight destinations on the ex-York & North Midland line towards Cudworth. As can be seen, there has been considerable rationalisation but a rail-served freight depot, operated by Cobra Railfreight, has been built. Kirkgate station is now provided with three platform faces and the original building survives. Two engineering sidings occupy part of the old goods yard. **(A2605-47/673506)**

WALSALL

Then: 27 June 1961
Now: 16 August 1997

This view, looking north, shows the complex approaches to Walsall from the Bescot direction. Visible is the ex-LNWR line from Bescot northwards through Walsall station. To the right (east) of the line is the ex-Midland Railway goods yard, whilst to the left (west) is the ex-LNWR goods yard. The line can be seen running through the station on towards Ryecroft Junction, where the route split four-ways, heading towards Wolverhampton (ex-MR), Rugeley (ex-LNWR), Lichfield (ex-LNWR) and Sutton Coldfield (ex-MR).

Although there was a station bearing the name Walsall prior to the opening of the line northwards from Bescot, this was some distance from the town. The line from Bescot, which eventually passed to the LNWR, was opened to a temporary terminus at Bridgeman Place on 1 November 1847; the line was extended northwards to

226

Wichnor via Lichfield on 9 April 1849, at which time a new station was opened. The line from Ryecroft Junction to Cannock was opened on 1 February 1858. The lines which were eventually to be operated by the Midland Railway opened westwards to Wolverhampton on 1 November 1872 and eastwards to Castle Bromwich on 1 July 1879.

Walsall suffered badly during the Beeching era. Already, on 5 January 1931, passenger services over the ex-MR route to Wolverhampton had been withdrawn. Passenger services were withdrawn from the Dudley-Walsall route on 6 July 1964. This was followed by the withdrawal of passenger services from Wolverhampton via the LNWR route and Pleck Junction (to the south of Walsall station) to Walsall and thence to Castle Bromwich on 18 January 1965. At the same time passenger services were withdrawn over the lines to Rugeley, via Cannock, and Wichnor Junction. Although these lines lost passenger services, all were to remain open for freight — at least in

the short term — with the exception of the ex-MR line towards Wolverhampton, which was closed completely beyond Birchills power station on 28 September 1964. However, the early 1980s saw two closures: the line serving Birchills power station closed completely on 12 May 1980 and that running north to Anglesea Sidings followed on 19 March 1984.

Today, Walsall sees electric services running to Birmingham New Street. These were introduced on 6 December 1966. The station at Walsall was rebuilt in 1980 as part of the Saddlers shopping centre but both the ex-LNWR and ex-MR goods yards have closed. On a more positive note, Walsall to Hednesford was reopened to passenger services, using DMUs, on 7 April 1989. This line has subsequently been extended a further four miles to Rugeley Town and plans exist for a further extension to link in with the West Coast main line at Rugeley. Also still extant is the ex-MR line from Walsall to Castle Bromwich, which remains freight only. (**A91587/670382**)

227

WATERLOO

Then: 30 April 1960
Now: 28 July 1997

Looking north across the River Thames, the overall roof of Charing Cross station can be seen on the north bank of the river whilst Waterloo station can be seen dominating the foreground.

Charing Cross station owes its origins to the South Eastern Railway which promoted a line from London Bridge, via Waterloo, across the river. Work started in 1862 and the first trains operated into the new station on 11 January 1864. Beyond the station was built the 250-bedroom Charing Cross Hotel. The original station roof, designed by Sir John Hackshaw, collapsed on 5 December 1905; although the collapse was relatively slow (allowing all trains and passengers to be evacuated), some six people were killed. The roof illustrated here was the result of the rebuilding after the accident.

Waterloo station is more than a decade older than Charing Cross, dating originally back to 11 July 1848

when the London & South Western Railway opened its extension from the earlier terminus at Nine Elms. The first station was extended in 1860 with the opening of the 'Windsor' platforms at the north and, in 1864, a link was built into the newly opened South Eastern Railway route from Charing Cross to London Bridge (although this was relatively shortlived and closed on 26 March 1911); Waterloo Junction (Waterloo East from 2 May 1977) was opened on 1 January 1869. The station as visible here was the result of rebuilding from 1909 onwards; the completed station, with war memorial to the dead of the LSWR in World War 1 and Victory Arch, was officially opened on 21 March 1922. The station layout, along with the famous signalbox, was the result of work in the mid-1930s. At the time of the 'Then' photograph, main line steam was still running from Waterloo and a rebuilt Bulleid Pacific is visible as is an 'M7' 0-4-4T. At this time Waterloo could

lay claim to 21 platforms; hidden by the station is the Armstrong lift, which provided access for rolling stock to and from the underground Waterloo & City line.

Today, the main train shed at Waterloo remains, although there have been further modifications — including the conversion of the former cab road into additional platforms as part of the plan to use Waterloo as the London terminus for cross-Channel trains. A modern replacement for the steam-hauled main line services, a 'Wessex Electric' EMU can be seen in the station, along with a range of other EMUs now operated by South West Trains. There are, however, major changes. Of these the most obvious is the completion of Nicholas Grimshaw's

dramatic 400m long overall roof for Waterloo International; the five-platform International station was opened in 1994 and four Eurostar rakes can be seen in the station. The construction of the International platforms required the demolition of the original 'Windsor' platforms, the removal of the Armstrong lift, the building of a new viaduct linking the new platforms with International Junction and the demolition of the 1930s signalbox. Work is also in hand for the construction of the Jubilee Line extension. Across the river, Charing Cross has also undergone a further rebuild, with a dramatic office block built over the country end of the platforms. (**A80041/669441**)

WATFORD JUNCTION

Then: 22 April 1953
Now: 1 October 1997

Situated on the West Coast main line, Watford Junction was the point where London & North Western Railway branches diverged eastwards to St Albans and westwards to Croxley Green and Rickmansworth. From the westernmost terminal platforms suburban trains served Watford High Street before rejoining the WCML at Bushey; these lines were also used by Bakerloo Line trains. As can be seen, Watford Junction was provided with extensive facilities, with five through roads serving the WCML as well as a branch platform for the line to St Albans and four terminal roads for suburban services. To the north of Watford, can be seen Watford Fast tunnel (on the westernmost set of lines) and the slightly longer Watford Slow tunnel (on the easternmost).

Watford was first served by the railway with the opening of the first section of the London & Birmingham

230

Railway (from Euston to Boxmoor) on 20 June 1837. This was followed by the opening of the branch to St Albans on 5 May 1858. The Rickmansworth branch (with the station at Watford High Street) opened on 1 October 1862. The West Coast main line was quadrupled in 1879. The branch to Croxley Green followed on 15 June 1912 in connection with the construction of an electrified duplicate route to Bushey thence to London. Services over the new route southwards commenced on 10 February 1913. Bakerloo trains started to operate to Watford on 16 April 1917 when the electrified route through to Watford was completed. The Croxley Green branch was electrified on 30 October 1922.

Today Watford Junction remains an important station on the now-electrified West Coast main line — with full services at 25kV starting between Euston and Rugby on 2 January 1966 (although the line had been energised earlier, in July 1965, with trains being electric-hauled north of Willesden). Passenger services continue to operate to St Albans and over the third-rail suburban line through High Street and Bushey, although those to Rickmansworth have been withdrawn and those to Croxley Green have been reduced to one early morning return working (operated by bus as part of the North London Lines franchise). Bakerloo services ceased to operate to Watford on 4 October 1982. One of the through roads at Watford Junction, the westernmost, has disappeared and the station has been rebuilt. The goods shed and long carriage shed have disappeared, as has the shed (coded 1C) which was situated in the triangle formed by the up slow platform and the St Albans branch platform in the 'Then' photograph. (**A48783/671997**)

WELWYN
(GARDEN CITY)

Then: 2 September 1959
Now: October 1997

In the early years of the 20th century a number of 'garden cities' emerged; one of these was Welwyn Garden City in Hertfordshire. This enterprise was started by a private concern in 1919 but taken over by the state after World War 2, the population of the town increasing 20 fold between 1921 and 1951. Originally Welwyn was served by a halt (opened on 16 August 1920) on the single-track branch to Luton, but this was replaced with the main line station illustrated on 20 September 1926. The junction for the branch westwards to Luton is obscured by the road overbridge immediately to the north of the station. Heading east slightly further to the north are the remains of the branch to Hertford, which lost its passenger services on 18 June 1951; a stub remained at the Welwyn end until the 1980s. In the far distance can be seen the double-track Welwyn Viaduct with Welwyn North station

beyond. This section remains today the only section of the East Coast main line between London and Stevenage not to be four-track and continues to cause capacity problems.

Welwyn's importance as a commuter town continues to grow. The station remains largely unchanged, although it has now gained a flyover to the south (in connection with the suburban electrification scheme it was completed in May 1975). There are few traces of the closed branch lines to Luton and Hertford, although the sidings to the southeast of the station remain. (**A78547/672328**)

WEYMOUTH

Then: 26 July 1957
Now: 15 August 1997

The Dorset town of Weymouth was both an important holiday resort and a significant ferry terminal for services to the Channel Islands and the continent. The quay serving the ferries can be seen on the extreme left of the 'Then' photograph (1). This was rail served by the famous quay line, which ran from the station area from the point (2) adjacent to the junction for the branch to Portland (3). The Portland branch can be seen crossing Radipole Lake having passed through the single platform of Melcombe Regis station (4). Westham Halt was situated on the west side of the bridge. The main ex-GWR/LSWR station is visible in the middle (5) with its extensive freight facilities and carriage sidings; the station illustrated here had only recently at this date been enlarged and a new signalbox installed (6).

The first railway to serve Weymouth was the broad gauge route from the north (converted to standard gauge in 1874), which was extended southwards through Dorchester

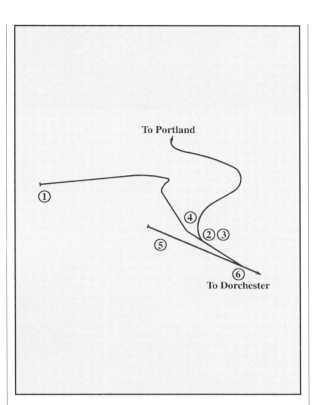

To Portland

① ④ ② ③ ⑤ ⑥

To Dorchester

— which had been served by trains from the east since 1847 — on 20 January 1857. The broad gauge route was to form part of the GWR's network and the Southern exercised running powers to gain access to the town. The quay line, originally horse-powered, was opened by the Weymouth & Portland Railway on 16 October 1865. The quay was built to mixed gauge but it was not until 1889 that the GWR ran its first boat train over the line (having taken over the Weymouth & Channel Islands Co). The Weymouth & Portland Railway was leased to the GWR and LSWR; its route to Portland was opened on 16 October 1865 and the viaduct illustrated here was built in 1909 replacing an earlier wooden structure.

In the 40 years since the 'Then' photograph was taken there have been many changes. Despite the presence of the Royal Navy at Portland, the branch had closed to passenger services on 3 March 1952 (although the spur serving Melcombe Regis platform was retained until 14 September 1959) with freight being withdrawn on 5 April 1965. Although the embankment of the now closed route can be seen stretching into the distance, the alignment over Radipole Lake has been replaced by a road bridge. In Weymouth itself, the station was rebuilt in 1986 and semaphore signalling was replaced in September the following year. Electric services to Weymouth were inaugurated in May 1988 and one of the five-car EMUs can be seen in the station. The freight facilities and carriage sidings have also largely disappeared, although the (mothballed) quay line remains. **(A68433/670464)**

WHITBY

Then: 9 June 1965
Now: 3 November 1997

The North Riding fishing port of Whitby is famous for its role in the Dracula story; it is also famous as the location for a 7th century Synod when the English church determined how Easter would be calculated. The ruined abbey (1), which is situated in a dominant clifftop position, can be seen adjacent to the church of St Mary's (2). The railway station (3), with a four-car DMU in one of the platforms, can be seen on the north side of the River Esk. There is also evidence of the freight traffic to the town in the adjacent goods yard. The former engine shed (4), which was closed in 1960 is still standing. Although the first railway to reach Whitby was the Whitby & Pickering, which opened in 1836, the present station, designed by G. T. Andrews, dates from the late 1840s.

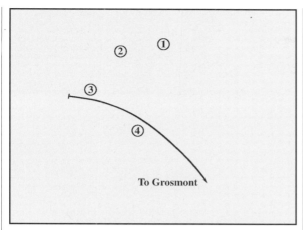

It was fitted, until 1952, with an overall roof but this was replaced with the platform awnings illustrated in this view. Not visible in this view is the line linking the Whitby-Grosmont route with the line from Saltburn to Scarborough that served Whitby West Cliff station and the viaduct that takes this latter route over the Esk about a mile south of the town.

Although the line linking Whitby with Grosmont (and ultimately Middlesbrough) was threatened with closure, it has survived (unlike the Saltburn-Scarborough and Grosmont-Pickering lines). Rationalisation has, however, been the order of the day. The railway has been reduced to a basic passenger facility and the harbour-front sidings have all disappeared. The massive growth in leisure sailing is apparent with a large number of yachts moored in the harbour. The old engine shed, however, has survived. (A152959/672593)

Viewed looking east towards Wick Bay, the town of Wick straddles the estuary of the Wick River. An important fishing port and regional centre, Wick was connected to the railway network with the opening of the long Highland Railway line from Helmsdale on 28 July 1874. For a period — from opening on 1 July 1903 through to complete closure on 3 April 1944 — Wick was also the northern terminus of the Wick & Lybster Light Railway. The facilities provided at Wick can be seen clearly in this view. The station building, with its overall roof, is surrounded by sidings full of freight stock. The two-road engine shed, coded 60D by British Railways, can be seen with two Stanier Class 5 4-6-0s

awaiting their next duty in front of it. Also visible is the turntable beyond the shed. Wick shed lost its steam allocation in July 1962, although it remained a stabling point for Inverness-based diesel locomotives thereafter.

Today, Wick retains its passenger services; although these have been threatened with closure (most notably in the Beeching Report), social considerations have ensured that the line to Wick, like those to Thurso, Kyle of Lochalsh, Mallaig and Oban, retain passenger services. Freight, too, continues to serve Wick. As can be seen, the station with its trainshed remains today, although both the engine shed and the turntable have disappeared. **(R23946/675413)**

WIGAN

Then: 13 March 1959
Now: 9 March 1998

The Lancashire town of Wigan was at the centre of one of the most important coalfields in the country; it was also, as shown in this 'Then' photograph (which is taken looking almost due northwest), the possessor of a complicated railway network, that saw services provided by three of the pre-Grouping companies — the Great Central, the Lancashire & Yorkshire and the London & North Western. In the foreground (1) can be seen the ex-GCR Central station; this was the terminus of a branch from Hindley. The ex-GCR goods yard was located slightly to the south of the area illustrated. Further west we see the ex-LYR Wigan Wallgate station (2). There is a junction (3) where the ex-LYR line heads eastwards towards Manchester and there is a connection up to the ex-LNWR route from Warrington. From Wigan Wallgate, the ex-LYR line headed northwestwards towards Southport (4) or westwards towards Liverpool (5). The ex-LNWR Wigan North Western station is situated slightly to the west of the area illustrated, but the line from the stattion can be seen heading north towards Preston.

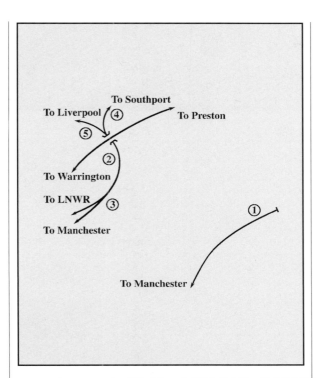

The first railway to serve Wigan was a branch off the Liverpool & Manchester Railway, from Parkside, which opened on 3 September 1832. This line was extended northwards to Preston, courtesy of the North Union Railway (later LNWR), on 31 October 1838. The LYR line from Liverpool through Wigan to Bolton opened on 20 November 1848; this was followed by the line to Southport, which opened on 9 April 1855. The final arrival was the GCR, which opened to a temporary station in Wigan on 1 April 1884 and thence to Wigan Central, as illustrated here, on 3 October 1892.

Although both Wigan Wallgate and Wigan North Western remain open, and passenger services continue to operate over the ex-LYR lines between Bolton and Liverpool or Southport and over the West Coast main line, Wigan Central is no more. Passenger services were withdrawn over the line from Wigan Central, via Glazebrook, to Manchester Central on 2 November 1964 and the GC presence in Wigan ceased with the closure of the line to the ex-GCR goods yard on 6 November 1967. The ex-LNWR West Coast main line through Wigan was electrified as part of the scheme to electrify the line from Crewe to Glasgow and electric services between Crewe and Preston were inaugurated on 23 July 1973. As can be seen today, all traces of the ex-GCR lines have disappeared, but much else remains intact.
(A74415/673489)

WINDSOR

Then: 26 June 1964
Now: 14 September 1996

The familiar view of Windsor, dominated at the centre by the castle, also shows clearly the juxtaposition of the two stations — the ex-London & South Western Railway Riverside to the right and the ex-Great Western Railway Central on the left.

In the competition to serve Windsor, the GWR was to win; its line, the short branch from Slough, opened on 8 October 1849. The ex-GWR line approaches Windsor over an embankment and a 202ft long bridge over the River Thames. Originally the approaches to the bridge were constructed of wood, but this was later replaced by the brick structure visible in this photograph. Originally constructed to Brunel's broad gauge, the line was converted to mixed gauge in 1862 and to standard gauge alone in 1883, at which time Central station was rebuilt. The station was further rebuilt, incorporating the royal waiting room, in 1897 — the year of Queen Victoria's Golden Jubilee — and again was further modified in 1907.

The LSWR, under the auspices of the Windsor, Staines & South Western Railway, lost the race to Windsor — but only just. Its line from Richmond was opened as far as Datchet on 22 August 1848 and thence to Riverside station on 1 December 1849. The LSWR, however, provided Windsor with a much more impressive station than that originally provided by the GWR. Designed by Sir William Tite, the station was constructed in red brick in a Tudor-Gothic style, that incorporated a curved trainshed.

Today, both Central and Riverside retain their passenger services, although freight is now a thing of the past for both routes. Riverside station has seen a reduction in the number of platforms, with the building of a modern office block on part of the site; passenger services today are in the hands of the Class 455 EMUs of South West Trains. Central, on the other hand, has seen its facilities much reduced. The old royal waiting room and associated trainshed were converted into the now-defunct 'Royalty and Empire' exhibition in 1981 by Madame Tussauds,

whilst the surviving passenger services were concentrated on to a single platform in the old terminus. Recently, permission has been granted for the line into Central to be foreshortened and the existing Central station site to be redeveloped.

One other dramatic change in the past 30 years has been the phenomenal growth in air traffic; Air Traffic Control constraints and the vagaries of the climate have precluded obtaining a precisely angled comparison shot, but this vertical view shows well the juxtaposition of the two stations as well as the single track approach to Central station. The curve of Riverside station   trainshed roof is also clearly visible alongside the offices.
(A132653/AF-96C/593 4731)

Then: 1957
Now: 1 October 1997

Served by the London & South Western Railway, Woking is now one of the most important commuter stations serving the privatised South West Trains. The 'Then' photograph gives a good impression of the facilities at the station in the late 1950s; although there is some third-rail evident, main line services to the southwest and south coast were still in the hands of steam and, as can be seen, tank engines were still in use for shunting. The freight facilities were significant. In the distance can be seen the Woking Homes, which were established for the orphans and pensioners of the LSWR (this building has been subsequently demolished and replaced with more modern accommodation). It was to Woking that the train that officially inaugurated services over the first section of the London & Southampton Railway ran on 19 May 1838. The line was extended to Winchfield on 24 September 1838. Woking's importance grew with the opening of the line to Guildford, which opened on 5 May 1845 and which was eventually extended to Portsmouth (the 'Portsmouth Direct' line). The line through Woking and Guildford was electrified before World War 2, with full services commencing on 3 January 1937.

As is evident, much of Woking has been rebuilt over the past 40 years; the station, however, remains largely unchanged, although it has gained a new island platform (which opened during 1997) at the London end of the central island platform. Elsewhere it is evident that there has been a considerable decline in the level of freight traffic. There remain a number of stone terminals and Woking also acts as a base for engineering work. Visible is a solitary Class 455 EMU. **(A74969/672020)**

WOLVERHAMPTON

Then: June 1938
Now: 16 August 1997

This view shows in some detail the east end of the ex-London & North Western High Level station in Wolverhampton. No less than five steam locomotives can be seen — one approaching the station with a service from the Birmingham direction, three in the station itself and one shunting the goods yard. Wolverhampton, like Stafford illustrated earlier, was one of the intermediate stations on the Grand Junction Railway which opened on

4 July 1837; the original GJR station in Wolverhampton was situated at Wednesfield Heath. The station was relocated to the present site on 24 June 1852, at which time the original station was renamed Wednesfield Heath. The new station was originally known as 'General' but was rechristened 'Queen Street' in 1853, only becoming 'High Level' on 1 June 1885. The station as illustrated in the 'Then' photograph was the result of a reconstruction in

1884. Apart from handling LNWR trains, High Level also served Midland Railway trains from the Walsall direction.

Although there were efforts to get High Level station rebuilt in the 1930s, nothing was undertaken until the scheme to electrify the West Coast main line commenced. The rebuilding of High Level station was announced in January 1962. Work started on the reconstruction on 19 February 1964. The station's overall roof was demolished on 22 February 1965 and the original facade followed on 11 January 1966. The new station was largely complete in time for the inauguration of electric services through High Level on 6 March 1967. The

'Now' view shows the east end of High Level station today, although with the closure of the adjacent ex-GWR Low Level, it is now known simply as 'Wolverhampton'. In the foreground, overlooking the station throat, can be seen the power box, which was commissioned on 18 August 1965. The goods yard has gone and there have also been dramatic changes in the background with very few buildings surviving from 60 years ago. In the bay platform waits a three-car EMU for a service towards Birmingham and Coventry whilst a Class 37 in EWS livery stands stabled close to the power box. **(57485/672060)**

WOLVERTON

Then: 2 November 1971
Now: 4 September 1997

Although this is one of the most recent 'Then' photographs in the book, there are still a number of quite striking changes that have occurred in the past 25 years. Wolverton is situated on the West Coast main line and the station can be seen in the right background. In the foreground can be seen the triangular junction for the ex-

LNWR branch to Newport Pagnell; this line had already, on 7 September 1964, seen its passenger services withdrawn and had been cut back from Newport Pagnell to Triangle ground frame on 22 May 1967 (the final section — from Wolverton South to Triangle ground frame — was closed on 15 October 1973). The WCML through

248

Wolverton opened courtesy of the London & Birmingham Railway in 1838 and the branch to Newport Pagnell followed on 2 September 1867. From 1887 until 1926, Wolverton was also served by a 3ft 6in gauge steam tramway that linked the town with Stony Stratford; this route was eventually owned by the LNWR, but no traces survived to be illustrated in the 'Then' photograph.

As Wolverton was approximately halfway between London and Birmingham, the L&BR selected it as the base for its locomotive workshops and these opened in 1838 as well. The population of the area, which had been less than 500 before the arrival of the railway, quickly grew. As the future LNWR expanded, Wolverton became the main locomotive repair depot of the southern section of the railway; however, in 1861 all locomotive work was transferred to Crewe and from 1865 Wolverton concentrated on carriage and wagon work. From 1962

Wolverton has specialised in carriage repair work, including handling the stock for the Royal Train. The station illustrated in the 'Then' shot dates from 1881 when the WCML was realigned to the east of its original route to allow for expansion of the works. Full electric services over the WCML through Wolverton started on 3 January 1966, although electric-hauled trains (to the old steam timetables) had operated from the previous year.

Today Wolverton remains both as a station and as a carriage works, although the latter activity is much reduced even from the level of 25 years ago — witness the rusting tracks — and the station has been rebuilt. Gone is the 1881-built main building on the road overbridge to be replaced with a new footbridge and more rudimentary facilities. All traces of the Newport Pagnell branch have gone, although the triangle can still be clearly seen. (**A221019/673594**)

WORCESTER

Then: 18 June 1934
Now: 16 August 1997

Worcester possesses two stations — Shrub Hill and Foregate Street — although only the extreme northern ends of the former are illustrated. The photograph, however, shows in detail the area of the triangle to the north of Shrub Hill, where the line towards Hereford, through Worcester Foregate Street, diverges from the old Oxford, Worcester & Wolverhampton line towards Droitwich. Dominating the scene in the centre is the local gas works; the sign at the west end of the complex reads 'GAS FOR ECONOMY'. In the centre of the triangle is Worcester's locomotive shed. The junction above the two gas holders is Rainbow Hill, whilst that beyond the locomotive shed towards Birmingham is Tunnel Junction. The first railway in the vicinity — the Birmingham & Gloucester (later part of the Midland) bypassed Worcester, although the Midland was later to get access to

250

the city by exercising running powers to Shrub Hill over the line from Abbot's Wood Junction from 1852 onwards. It was the OWW that brought railways to the city; the first section, from Shrub Hill to Abbot's Wood Junction opening on 5 October 1850. This was followed by the line north to Droitwich on 18 February 1852. The OWW was extended southwards to Evesham from Norton Junction on 1 May 1852. Both the OWW and the later Worcester & Hereford were to become part of the GWR. The W&H line from Henwick, on the city's outskirts, through Foregate Street, to Tunnel Junction opened on 17 May 1860; until the Rainbow Hill Junction-Shrub Hill curve opened on 25 July 1860, trains to and from Shrub Hill towards Foregate had to reverse at Tunnel Junction. Also visible in the photograph running from the Rainbow

Hill-Shrub Hill curve is the 'Vinegar Works Branch', which served the factory of Hill Evans & Co. This line opened in 1872 and was unusual in that motorists had to obey GWR-style lower quadrant signals at two level crossings.

Worcester retains its two stations, although the locomotive shed and goods yard have now disappeared. Rainbow Hill Junction was abolished in the 1970s, when the lines through to Henwick were treated as two single lines. Tunnel Junction, however, still survives as does its 1905-built signalbox. In the foreground can be seen the platforms of Shrub Hill station. The gas works has also disappeared although the impressive industrial site in front of it remains. The 'Vinegar Works Branch' closed in 1964. (**44988/670342**)

WREXHAM

Then: 3 April 1963
Now: 9 September 1997

In the foreground can be seen the lines of the ex-Great Western Shrewsbury-Chester route. More prominent, however, in the centre of the photograph is Wrexham Central station. This was the point where the Great Central (as operator of the Wrexham, Mold & Connah's Quay Railway) met the Cambrian Railways' line from Ellesmere. The half-mile section of WM&CQR line that ran under the GWR route and served Wrexham Central

was built to serve the new station, which opened on 1 November 1887. The WM&CQR's original terminus at Wrexham was renamed 'Exchange'. The Wrexham & Ellesmere line was incorporated on 31 July 1885, but no work started until seven years later and was not opened until 2 November 1895. It was operated at the outset by the Cambrian Railways and thus eventually passed to the Great Western Railway. In this photograph it is possible to

make out a two-car DMU in the station awaiting a departure towards Shotton and the Wirral peninsula.

Today, the once well-provided station at Wrexham Central is no more, having been reduced to a single platform and even this is destined to disappear with the recently approved closure of a short section of track. A new station will be constructed closer to the ex-GWR Chester-Shrewsbury line. Passenger services over the line to Ellesmere were withdrawn on 10 September 1962 and the line was progressively cut back for freight until the final section, from Wrexham Central to the sidings at Abenbury, was closed on 4 May 1981. Despite the relatively recent demise of this last section of line, it is difficult to trace the route of the track beyond the somewhat desolate Central station. (**A109169/671552**)

YORK

Then: 21 June 1961
Now: 22 October 1997

It is only from the air that we can get a true feeling for how great an impact the railways have had on the landscape. York, one of Britain's most ancient cities, was dominated to the west of the historic core by the arrival of the railways. Here it is almost possible to see the old station (1), which dated back to 1839 and a rebuilding of 1841 and which, at this time, housed the York Railway Museum. The new station (2) was authorised in July 1866 and was constructed from 1874, opening formally on 25 June 1877. In the distance can be seen the lines to Harrogate (3) and Thirsk (4) heading away from the city. York North shed (5) was much rebuilt during the 1950s and, along with the Leeman Road goods shed (6), now forms the National Railway Museum (opened in 1975). The Queen Street Workshops (7) are sited to the south of the station; other workshops are those handling carriages

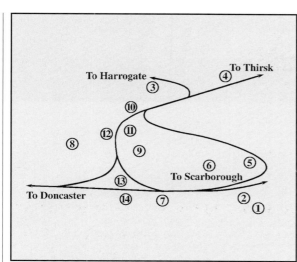

(8) and wagons (9). Also visible are the North Yard (10), Up Yard (11) and Down Yard (12) as well as York South shed (13) and Queen Street shed (14).

As can be seen, although York remains a major railway centre, much has changed. The track, particularly in the station area, has been rationalised with the arrival of the 25kV East Coast main line electrification. After much controversy, the National Railway Museum has acquired a new roof following concern about the stability of the 1950s structure. The South Shed was demolished in 1963 and the Queen Street shed followed in 1974. The former wagon works survives for maintenance and repair work although it was closed as a workshop in 1965. Also now closed, after having been privatised, is the Carriage Works; following the completion of orders for EMUs the workshops closed in August 1996. However, the recent upturn in the railway freight business has seen part of the site pass to an American concern and the new owner is planning to build wagons here. (A91490/672594)

255

AEROFILMS

Aerofilms was founded in 1919 and has specialised in the acquisition of aerial photography within the United Kingdom throughout its history. The company has a record of being innovative in the uses and applications of aerial photography.

Photographs looking at the environment in perspective are called oblique aerial photographs. These are taken with Hasselblad cameras by professional photographers experienced in the difficult conditions encountered in aerial work.

Photographs looking straight down are termed vertical aerial photographs. These photographs are obtained using Leica survey cameras, the products from which are normally used in the making of maps.

Aerofilms has a unique library of oblique and vertical photographs in excess of one and a half million in number covering the United Kingdom. This library of photographs dates from 1919 and is being continually updated.

Oblique and vertical photography can be taken to customers' specification by Aerofilms' professional photographers.

To discover more of the wealth of past or present photographs held in the library at Aerofilms or to commission new aerial photographs, please contact:

Aerofilms Ltd
Gate Studios
Station Road
Borehamwood
Herts
WD6 1EJ

Telephone: 0181 207 0666
Fax: 0181 207 5433